more FAITH FACTS for Young Catholics

Fun Ways to Teach the Basics of Our Faith

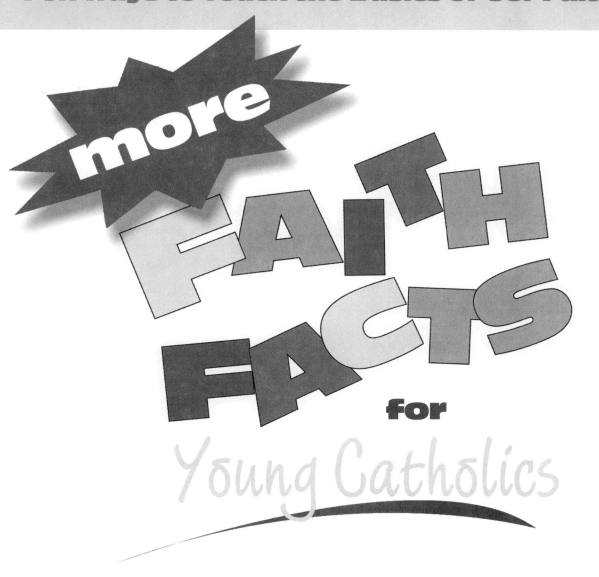

more
FAITH
FACTS
for
Young Catholics

Kieran Sawyer, s.s.n.d.

ave maria press   Notre Dame, IN

A special thanks to the Faith-a-thon Committee of the Archdiocese of Milwaukee who helped to develop the four hundred study cards: Barb Abler, Kathie Amidei, Ellen Heitman, Kayon Henning, Shelly McGuine, and Shelly Schwingle.

Some of the questions used in the "Gospel Trivia Cards" (pages 161-164) appeared in *Risk of Faith* (Ave Maria Press, 1988).

The "Catechism Categories Game" (pages 36-39) was prepared by Sr. Ellen Jean Klein, S.S.N.D.

International Standard Book Number: 0-87793-947-0

Cover design by Brian Conley

Text design by Kathy Coleman and Brian Conley

Printed and bound in the United States of America.

Library of Congress Cataloging-in-Publication Data

Sawyer, Kieran.

    More faith facts for young Catholics : fun ways to teach the basics of our faith / Kieran Sawyer.

        p. cm.

    ISBN 0-87793-947-0

    1. Catholic Church--Doctrines. 2. Church work with young adults. 3. Catholic Church--Education. 4. Christian education of adults. I. Title.

BX1751.2 .S363   2000

268'.82--dc21

                                                  00-008682

                                                  CIP

Contents

Introduction

At the time of the publication of my book *Faith Facts for Young Catholics* (1998) I mentioned that the teaching and drilling of information that involves our faith should play an important but subsidiary role in every religious education situation. In the time since then I have traveled around the country giving workshops and talks based on the book. I am even more convinced of the need for young people to spend more time and energy learning the factual data of their faith.

However, since the publication of the first book, an interesting aside has emerged. It seems that many "older" children—up to junior high and high school age—also have found the drilling of facts about faith and religion useful. Hence, a follow-up. In *More Faith Facts for Young Catholics* I have provided some more essential information that *all* Catholics should know along with some simple, fun, creative, and exciting games, drills, and activities that will enliven any religion class or religious education setting.

Once again, I must emphasize that I am not advocating that memorization supplant the more contemporary process of storytelling, discussion, reflection, and prayerful experiences that are so much a part of effective religious education. But I remain convinced that today's young people (and all Catholics) need to spend more time and energy learning the factual data of their faith.

Really knowing the facts of faith gives young people the vocabulary they need to think and talk about deeper matters of faith. A facile knowledge of the faith facts is an important component in developing for them a sense of Catholic identity. The facts also provide a structure within which they can organize the vast array of truths that make up church doctrine and church tradition. To repeat an old phrase I learned from my father, memorized facts provide "pegs to hang your knowledge on."

Creative Gaming

It is my experience that the best way to teach faith facts to students is through creative, exciting learning games. This book presents many such games that can be used in a variety of religious education settings: religion classes in school or CCD, youth group meetings, and youth retreats. You may also wish to refer to my first book, *Faith Facts for Young Catholics*, for other learning games and variations.

The use of games to teach religious facts should be guided by several important principles:

Principle 1: Everyone Pays Attention Learning games should be structured to keep every person *engaged* in the learning process. Everyone should be able to see and hear the entire activity. The team that is not "up" should be learning as well as the team that is. The persons not called on should be thinking along with the one who is. If the class should become unruly or disrespectful, stop the game, review the rules, and begin again. If that fails, change to a quiet writing activity.

Principle 2: Every Minute Is Learning Time Keep the mechanics of the game simple so that as much time as possible is spent in actual learning. Study the directions for the game in advance so that you are sure you know how to play it. Ask questions in such a way that they themselves are part of the learning process. Give clues to keep a game from bogging down when someone doesn't know the answer. Use time between rounds or games to study or review. Keep a supply of study cards and flash cards in a prominent place and encourage students to study them together before class and at breaks.

Principle 3: Everyone Is a Winner Learning games should be planned so that every student feels that he or she is succeeding. Avoid situations that always allow the brighter youngster to win. Avoid choosing sides in a way that would leave the slower student to be chosen last. Pay special attention to problem students, giving them extra clues, allowing them to shuffle cards, keep score, etc. Give reading roles to better readers who will not be embarrassed by mistakes. If a game is faltering because few people seem to know

the answers, stop for a few minutes of review and study time, then resume the game, or switch to one that is less challenging.

Principle 4: Everyone Works Together While learning games need a certain amount of competition to be enjoyable, the focus should be on cooperative learning rather than competition. Build up team spirit with cheers, chants, and small rewards for the winners. Encourage teams to cheer for their teammates and for other teams. Give teams time to review together, which encourages the brighter students to help the slower students review the content. Switch teams often, trying to keep them balanced, and giving the students a chance to work with all of their classmates.

Principle 5: Everyone Has Fun Learning games should be fun for the teacher as well as the students. Keep a positive, upbeat attitude. Use a game or two to liven up a difficult or dull lesson, or to reward the class for especially good behavior. Don't play any one game too long. Once the class has become acquainted with several of the games, allow them to choose the one they want to play. Do not allow cheating, booing, or other unsportsmanlike activities.

Learning Drills, Games, and Activities

Part One provides directions for many different kinds of drills, games, and activities.

The drills, games, and activities provide a variety of interesting and exciting ways to memorize, review, and drill factual material. Study the directions for each game in advance so that you are thoroughly familiar with how it is played and have all the necessary material needed for play. Once you are sure of how the games work, use them creatively, adapting them to your own situation, your time constraints, your students' interests, etc.

The games presented here are designed with middle school and junior high students in mind, however, many of them can be adapted for use with high school students or, oppositely, with younger children. Likewise, the games which are presented with specific content can be adapted for use with other content.

Resources

Part Two includes several reproducible resources that are used in the drills, activities, and games: study cards, outline sheets, key word cards, scripture study cards, and flash cards. These are described below.

Study Cards

Many of the learning games and drills require the use of **Study Cards**. The study cards are printed with a word or phrase on one side and a short definition or explanation on the other. They can be used in a game in both directions, so that either the word or the definition becomes the question and the opposite side the answer. The students can also be taught to use the study cards for individual study: looking at one side of the card, giving the answer mentally, turning the card over to check their answer, studying the card if they are wrong. Study cards can be used for individual study, small group or partner study, and large group drill games.

On pages 43 to 122 you will find 400 study cards, grouped in four sets: A, B, C, and D/L. Each set is progressively more difficult, with Set A containing 100 easier, more basic faith vocabulary words, Set B being a bit more difficult, and so forth. Set D/L contains eighty quite challenging vocabulary cards and twenty additional cards asking for lists, multiple answers, or prayers.

It is recommended that you select the study cards you want your students to learn or review and to make a set of cards for each person in your class. You may also wish to create additional cards for other important words or questions found in your religion textbook.

Duplicate the study cards on colored paper or card stock, using a different color for each set: e.g., green for set A, pink for set B, blue for set C, yellow for set D, and orange for set L. For longer wear, laminate the sheets or cover them with clear contact paper before cutting them apart. Package the cards in small zip lock bags, 6 1/2" x 3 3/4". (An easier option is to have the cards duplicated and cut at a local copy-making store, which typically costs just over one

dollar per set of 100 cards. Your students could do the collating and packaging.)

Outline Sheets and Key Word Cards

Some of the games require the use of **Outline Sheets** and **Key Word Cards**. Key word cards are words or phrases that are designed to be used with a particular learning activity. These might include books of the Bible, phrases from a prayer, events in history, parts of the Mass, and so forth. Key word cards can be used for individual or small group study as well as for games.

For example, in "Who, What, When" (page 26) the students learn to place significant events in Christian history on a time line. In "Bible Books Game" (page 31), the students place the names of the books of the Bible in categories shown on the outline sheet. You are encouraged to create similar sets of outlines and key words based on the content of your own class curriculum.

Scripture Study Cards

There are three kinds of scripture study cards. **Gospel Trivia Cards** and **Old Testament Trivia Cards** contain questions from the Old or New Testaments and the scriptural references where the answers can be found. Though these are called "trivia" cards, the questions have been written to teach concepts about scriptural events and persons that should be part of a young Christian's general knowledge. The suggested trivia games also give the students practice in looking up biblical passages.

The **Beatitude Cards** give part of a passage on one side of the card and the remainder of the passage on the other side. They can be used to help the students memorize well-known scripture passages.

You will want at least one set of each kind of scripture study cards for your class. Duplicate each set of cards in a different color. Laminate the sheets or cover them with clear contact paper before cutting them apart. Package them in small envelopes or zip lock bags.

Scripture study cards can be used for both individual study and games for small and large groups. Directions for playing learning games with the cards are found in Part One.

Flash Cards

Flash Cards are one-sided cards containing a word or short phrase printed large enough to be seen by everyone in the group. Flash cards can be used to present new vocabulary words, and for small group or large group drill and review.

There are 103 flash cards on pages 123-135. The cards, which are printed in alphabetical order, contain words which can be grouped into several categories: e.g., apostles, evangelists, New Testament women, and parables. See pages 16-19 for a listing of the categories and the flash cards in each. It is also recommended that you create flash cards for important words from your own religion text.

If possible, enlarge the flash cards found in this book, so that the cards you use with your class are about 3"x 8". Duplicate these on card stock. Laminate the sheets or cover them with clear contact paper before cutting them apart. You will need one or two sets of flash cards for your class.

Part 1

Drills, Games, and Activities

Study Card Tips

Tips for Individual Study

- Instruct the students to select ten **Study Cards (pages 43-122)** that they will need to master and to then organize the cards so they are all definition-side up.
- Have the students place the pack of cards on their desks. Instruct them to read the first definition, say the answer to themselves, then turn the card over to see if they were correct.
- If the person knew the answer, they should place the card in their KNOW pack. If they were wrong, or weren't sure, they should study the card a minute, then put it back at the bottom of their STUDY pack. If they don't understand the answer, or don't know what a word means, they should ask you (or another student) for help.
- Have the students continue through the pack until they have moved all of the cards into their KNOW pack.
- Next, have them turn the pack over so that the words are on top.
- They should pick the top card and read the word. In their mind, have them give a definition or explanation of the word, then turn the card over to see if they were correct. (The answer doesn't have to be word for word, but should contain all of the main ideas.)
- If they knew the answer, they should put the card in their KNOW pack; if not it should be put back at the bottom of their STUDY pack.
- When all of the cards have been moved into the KNOW pack, the student is ready to select ten more cards and repeat the entire process.

Pair Study

- Working with a partner, two students together select ten study cards that they both want to review.
- Person A takes the pack of cards and reads the first definition to Person B. If B knows the answer, B puts the card in the KNOW pack. If not, A shows B the card, helps B to study it, then puts it back at the bottom of the STUDY pack to be read again.
- When B has answered all of the questions correctly, B becomes the reader, reading the same set of cards to Person A.

- When both partners know all of the answers, select ten more study cards and repeat the process. This time Person B is the first reader.
- When the pair has twenty cards in their KNOW pack, they should turn the pack over so the words are on top. Take turns picking a card and giving the definition.

Small Group Study

- Divide the class into groups of four to six students.
- Give each group a set of ten to twenty study cards.
- Instruct the students to deal out the cards so that everyone gets several. The cards are passed slowly around the circle, giving everyone a chance to review them. Keep passing the cards until everyone is familiar with all of the cards
- Appoint one person in each group to be the reader. The reader collects all of the cards, then reads the definitions to the group, being careful so the word side of the cards doesn't show. The first person to name each word gets the card. In case of a tie, the card goes back into the reader's pack and is read again.
- The person who accumulates the most cards becomes the next reader.

Note: This game works only with one-word answers.

Team Study

- Divide the class into teams for any of the following games: Credo (page 35), Tic Tac Toe (page 20), Pick Your Pack.
- Before beginning play, tell the class which study cards you will be using and allow a few minutes for them to study together in preparation for the game. (You will often find the brighter students using this time to "drill" the slower members of their team, which is a very effective learning tool.)

Pick Your Pack

- Select a set of **Study Cards (pages 43-122)** to be reviewed. Divide the questions into three levels of difficulty. Mark three envelopes 3, 5, and 10 and place a pack of questions in each

envelope, the easier questions in 3, medium in 5, and harder in 10. You will need a set of three envelopes for each table.

- Divide the class into pairs. Seat three or four pairs at one table. Give each table a set of three envelopes, a scorecard, and a pencil. Designate a scorekeeper for each table.
- To begin play, Pair A decides what pack they want their question drawn from. Someone from Pair B draws the top card from that envelope and reads them the definition, being careful not to show them the word on the back. Pair A confers, then gives their answer. If they are correct, the points they earned are marked on the scorecard. If they are wrong, no points are scored. The question card just used is placed under the envelope.
- Pair B then chooses the pack they want their question drawn from. Someone from Pair C draws the top card from that envelope and reads it to them, and so on.
- When all of the cards from one envelope have been used up, pairs must choose from the remaining packs.

Option: You may want to assign pairs according to ability, so that all the pairs at a given table are somewhat evenly matched.

Flash Card Categories

- The Resource section contains 103 **Flash Cards (pages 123-135)**. The words on the flash cards can be arranged in several different categories (see pages 17-19) for individual, small group, and team study.
- Select one of the categories. Duplicate and cut one set of cards for that category for each student and one set for you.
- Prepare and present definitions for each word. Allow time for the students to study the words and review the definitions.
- After study time, hold up one of the words from your set so that all can see. Call on random students to tell you the definition. If the person has trouble, allow someone else to help.

Sample Flash Card Categories

Apostles
- Simon Peter
- Andrew
- James (the Greater)
- John
- Philip
- Bartholomew
- Thomas
- Matthew
- James (the Lesser)
- Thaddeus (Jude)
- Simon the Zealot
- Judas Iscariot

Evangelists
- Matthew
- Mark
- Luke
- John

Archangels
- Gabriel
- Michael
- Raphael

Biblical Places
- Bethany
- Bethlehem
- Cana
- Emmaus
- Galilee
- Jericho
- Jerusalem
- Nazareth
- Samaria

Gifts of the Holy Spirit
- Wisdom
- Understanding
- Knowledge
- Right Judgment
- Courage
- Reverence
- Wonder and Awe in God's Presence

New Testament Men
- Barabbas
- Herod
- Joachim
- John the Baptist
- Joseph of Arimathea
- Joseph of Nazareth
- Lazarus
- Nicodemus

Pilate

Saul

Zacchaeus

Zachary

New Testament Women

Anna

Elizabeth

Herodias

Joanna

Mary and Martha

Mary Magdalene

Mary Mother of James

Mary Mother of Jesus

Old Testament Men

Abraham

Adam

David

Goliath

Isaac

Jacob

Jonathon

Joshua

Noah

Samuel

Solomon

Old Testament Women

Bathsheba

Deborah

Esther

Eve

Judith

Leah

Miriam

Rachel

Rebecca

Ruth

Sarah

Parables

Good Samaritan

Lost Sheep

Mustard Seed

Pearl of Great Price

Prodigal Son

Sower and Seed

Ten Virgins

Wedding Feast

Prophets

Amos

Elisha

Isaiah

Jeremiah

Jonah

Nathan

Sacraments	*Titles for Jesus*
Baptism	Bread of Life
Confirmation	Emmanuel
Holy Eucharist	Good Shepherd
Reconciliation	Lamb of God
Anointing of the Sick	Light of the World
Holy Orders	Messiah
Matrimony	Son of God
	The Christ

Flash Card Games

There are several games that work well for large group study of the flash card words. They include: Large Group Tic Tac Toe Game (page 20), Musical Flash Cards (page 21), Who Am I? (page 22), and Untest (page 23).

Tic Tac Toe

Pairs Study Tic Tac Toe Game

- Divide the class into evenly matched pairs. Give each pair a set of **Study Cards (pages 43-122)** and a piece of paper. Instruct the pairs to arrange the cards so that they are all question side up and place them in a neat pack in front of them. Instruct them to draw a small tic tac toe grid on their paper.
- Person X picks the top card from the pack and reads the question to Person O. If Person O answers correctly, he or she puts an "O" in the grid. Person O then draws a card and reads the question to Person X. If Person X answers correctly, he or she places an "X" in the grid.
- When someone gives an incorrect answer, no "X" or "O" is marked and the question is placed at the bottom of the pack.
- Continue play until either Person X or Person O wins (gets 3 X's or O's in a row), or until there is a draw. Tally the win (or call a "cat's game"). Then draw another grid and play a second round.

Option: Allow the pairs to play this game at the chalkboard.

Large Group Tic Tac Toe Game

- Create a large tic tac toe grid on a sheet of poster board, making the blocks in the grid about six inches square.
- Create a set of X and O markers. (Cut ten four-inch squares out of tag board and write a large "X" on five of them and a large "O" on the other five.)
- Select a set of **Flash Cards (pages 123-135)** you want the group to review.
- Sit in a large circle and count off into two teams, alternating between Team X and Team O. Place the grid on the floor in the center of the circle and put the X markers and O markers in two piles near the grid. Then place one flash card *face down* in each square of the grid. (For an easier game, place the flash cards face up.)
- To begin play, one person on Team X picks up any flash card and attempts to identify it. If the answer is correct, the player

replaces the card with an X. If the answer is wrong, it is returned to its face-down position. The next person in the circle (who will be on Team O) then picks up a flash card and attempts to identify it. If the answer is correct, the player replaces the card with an O, and so on.

- The play continues around the circle until one team wins (gets 3 X's or 3 O's in a row), or until there is a draw. Tally the win or draw. Then replace the cards that have been removed with a new set of flash cards and begin a second round.
- Prompting by teammates is an automatic miss.

Musical Flash Cards

- Select a set of **Flash Cards (pages 123-135)** that you want to review. You will need at least one card for each member of the class.
- Write out for yourself a list of categories that match the cards selected: e.g., apostles, evangelists, New Testament women, Old Testament prophets, popes. A word can fit into more than one category. It is also possible for a category to have only one word: e.g., the current bishop of Rome.
- Create two score sheets on 8 1/2"x 11" paper, writing a large Team A across the top of one, Team B across the other. Attach the score sheets to clipboards.
- Prepare a tape or CD with some lively music.
- Instruct the class to sit in a large circle, then alternate counting off into two teams, Team A and Team B. Designate a scorekeeper from Team A to keep score for Team B, and vice versa. The scorekeepers sit on chairs inside the circle, holding the clipboards and a marking pen.
- Pass out the flash cards so that every player has one.
- Start the music. While the music is playing, the students pass their flash cards to the right.
- When the music stops, call out a category (e.g., apostles). All those who are holding a card that names an apostle should stand *immediately* and move to their team's scorekeeper. The scorekeeper, with the help of the group, checks to see if the

right people are standing. (No one is allowed to stand or sit down while the checking is going on.)

- The scorekeeper awards one point to each person standing who should be. The scorekeeper deducts one point for each person not standing who should be, one point for each person standing who should not be, or one point for any prompting by teammates.
- Repeat the process for as many rounds as desired. You may wish to change the scorekeeper each round.

Option: Insert several new cards each round. Do this by designating one person to be the "card exchanger." Give the card exchanger a stack of flash cards and instruct him or her to randomly remove one flash card and add another as the cards are being circulated.

Who Am I?

- Select a set of **Flash Cards (pages 123-135)** that name people, places, or things.
- Tape one flash card onto the back of each player, being careful that no one sees the card being put on his or her back.
- When all have a flash card taped on their backs, instruct the players to walk around the room, asking "yes or no" questions of their classmates (e.g., "Am I a woman?" or "Was I named in the New Testament?"). They may ask only three questions per person. The answers given must be limited to "yes" or "no."
- When a player has correctly identified the word on his or her back, he or she reports to the teacher, who removes the card.
- If all but two or three players have guessed their word, have everyone else work together giving them clues until they guess correctly.
- For a second round, use a new set of words or put the same words on the backs of different people.

Untest

- Prepare twenty questions with one word or short phrase answers from the **Flash Cards (pages 123-135)**.
- Instruct the students to number a piece of paper from 1 to 20.
- Read the first five questions one at a time, allowing just enough time for everyone to write the answers.
- Next allow two minutes of "cheat time." Tell the students that they are allowed to compare answers with those around them and to "fix" any answers they didn't have correct on their own.
- Give the correct answers, then ask for a show of hands to the following two questions: "Who had all the answers correct before 'cheat time'?" "Who got them right with some help from your friends?"
- Read the next five questions and repeat the process. Remind the students not to compare answers until you call for "cheat time."
- Later in the class, or at another session, repeat the test without allowing any cheat time.

Apostles' Creed Games

Preparation

- Create two types of sets of **Creed Cards (pages 137-140)**, sets A and B.
- For set A, duplicate both sides of the creed cards (creed phrases and explanations). You will need one set for every participant.
- For set B, duplicate the front side only of the creed cards. (You may wish to enlarge the type before duplication.) You will need just one set B for your entire class.

Creed Game 1

- Divide the class into groups of three participants each. Give each group one pack of set A creed cards. For this game you will only need one set for every three participants.

- Instruct the group to spread out the cards on the table (or floor) in front of them with all of the cards turned phrase side up. Then have them work together to put the cards in proper sequence order. When they are not sure of the sequence, they may check the sequence number on the back.
- The small group now takes turns: the first person explains what the first phrase means, then turns the card over to check the explanation given on the back. (Explanations do not have to be word-for-word.) The second person explains the second phrase, and so forth.
- When all twenty cards have been turned over, the small group repeats the process in reverse: each person reads the explanation given, gives the official creed phrase, and turns the card over to verify the answer. (Creed phrases should be given in exact wording.)
- Next tell the group to mix up the cards, keeping them phrase side up. When all have mixed the cards, have the groups race to see which group can put them in sequence order the fastest. Check with the sequence numbers on the back only when all cards are in order.
- For another round, have the groups mix up the cards, phrase side up, then select a representative to move to another table. When all reps are in place, call GO, and have the reps arrange the cards in sequence with the rest of the table watching. Repeat with other rounds, choosing a different representative each time.

 ## Creed Game 2

- Give each student a pack of set A creed cards. Instruct them to spread out the cards in the proper prayer sequence, using the sequence numbers on the back only if needed.
- When all students have the twenty cards correctly placed in front of them, recite the creed together, with the students turning over each card as it is recited.
- Instruct the students to collect their cards so they are all prayer phrase side up, then spend a few minutes studying quietly by flipping the cards one by one, trying to recite the next card before they reveal it.

- Divide the group into pairs. Person A holds a set of creed cards in correct sequence. Person B recites the creed, while Person A flips the cards as a check. Then Person B holds the cards and Person A recites. If either misses, he or she should spend some time studying from the pack, then try again.

Creed Game 3

- Give each person a pack of set A creed cards. Instruct the students to put the cards in proper sequence, creed phrase side up.
- Next instruct the students to study the meaning of each phrase by flipping through the pack, thinking what each phrase means, then turning the card over to check with the meaning given on the back.
- Reverse the above activity, starting with the explanation side, thinking of the creed phrase, then turning the card over to check.
- Play the game with a partner as in Creed Game 2.

Creed Game 4

- Use the pack of set B cards (creed phrases on the front and no sequence or explanation on the back) for this game. If you have fewer than twenty students, clip two adjoining cards together so that you have one card (or clipped set) for each student. If you have more than twenty students, have some of the students partner up to make twenty.
- Distribute the cards, putting them face down in front of the students. When all the cards have been distributed, call "Go." The students turn their cards over and arrange themselves in proper order, holding up the creed card(s) for all to see.
- For a second round, collect the cards, have everyone sit down, then redistribute them. This time use a stopwatch to see how long it takes the class to stand with the cards in order, beginning with the person with the first card. Repeat several rounds, working for a better time each round.
- Before sitting down after the last round, recite the creed, with everyone saying the phrase on the card(s) they are holding.

Who, What, When Presentation and Drills

Preparation

- Duplicate one copy of the **Who, What, When Time Line (pages 141 to 144)**. Cut the time line into strips and paste the strips in chronological order onto one long line. For better wear, cover the entire time line with clear contact paper.
- Duplicate the **Who, What, When Study Cards (pages 145-152)** with the events on one side and the dates on the back. Cut the sheets into separate cards, and put each set of ten in a separate envelope. (To make the drill games easier, copy each page on a different color paper.)
- Duplicate the **Who, What, When Date Sheet (pages 153-156)**, making one copy for each student.

Presentation

- Stretch the time line on the floor across the room. Have the students sit where they can all see it. Explain that each study card has a corresponding slot on the time line, with events shown in rectangles or bars and people shown in ovals.
- Randomly distribute the first ten study cards. Point to the first item on the time line, and ask the person who has the corresponding card to read the card aloud and then place it on the floor just above the strip. Do this with each of the first ten items.
- Distribute the second set of ten study cards, and proceed as above. Then do the same with the last two sets.
- Give everyone a copy of the date sheets, explaining that each item on the date sheets is also on one of the study cards. Allow a few minutes for the students to study the first ten items on the date sheet while you mix up the first ten cards on the floor. Then call out two or three volunteers to put the first ten cards back in order. Repeat this process with the other three sets.
- Repeat all four sets with other volunteers.

Who, What, When Drill 1

- Prepare a set of one-sided study cards. Do not include the side with the dates.
- Stretch the time line across the floor. Scatter the study cards on the floor just above the line, the first ten above the first section, and so on.
- Divide the class into four teams. Have each team kneel in front of one section of the line. When you say "Go," each team works together to put the cards in place on the line. The team stands when they are finished. Have the teams check each other's work using the date sheets. The first team to stand and have all answers right gets four points, the second three points, etc.
- Repeat this process four times, with the teams rotating to a different part of the time line each round. Total points determine the winning team.

Who, What, When Drill 2

- Stretch the time line across the floor. Put the first ten cards in one paper bag and the second ten cards in another bag. Place the bags about six feet back from the time line.
- Divide the students into two teams. Team A lines up behind the first bag, Team B behind the second. When you say GO, the first player from each team takes a card out of the bag, reads aloud the title (**bold** print only), runs to the time line, and puts the card in place on the line. He or she then comes back and tags the second player who also picks a card and runs to the line, and continues in the same order as before. Allow a player to correct any mistakes he or she sees on the line, but only when at the line.
- When all cards are in place, checkers from the opposite team compare the cards to the date sheets, removing any card that is out of place.
- Score one point for each correct answer on the line plus five points for the team that finished first.
- Teams exchange sides and repeat the game as above.
- Repeat the game with the third and fourth sets of cards. Total all rounds for a final winner.

Option: To make the game more difficult, use twenty cards at a time. For an ultimate game, use all forty cards. Time the teams to see who can complete the entire line in the least time.

Old Testament and Gospel Trivia

Preparation

- Duplicate and cut out the **Old Testament Trivia Cards (pages 157-160)** and the **Gospel Trivia Cards (pages 161-164)**.
- Both of the following games may be played with either one or both of the sets of trivia cards. A combined game of Old Testament Trivia and Gospel Trivia will be harder if both sets are duplicated on the same color paper and easier if different colors are used.
- All the participants need their own bibles for these games. *The New American Bible with Revised New Testament* was used to prepare the questions for this game. If you are not using this version, check the questions to make sure the scripture references are the same.

Trivia Game 1

- Divide the class into groups of eight, and subdivide each group into two teams, Team A and Team B. Have them sit in a circle. As much as possible the teams should be evenly matched in terms of their knowledge of scripture. Assign a "reader" for each team.
- Place a pack of trivia cards face down in the center of each group.
- To begin play, the reader on Team A draws a trivia card from the pack, quietly tells his or her own team where the answer can be found, and reads the question to Team B. The members of Team B confer about the answer without using their bibles. While Team B is conferring, the members of Team A are looking up the answer in their bibles. When Team B is ready, their reader says, "The answer is. . . . " If the answer is correct, the trivia card is placed in a "correct" pile in front of Team B. If the answer is wrong, the question is placed at the bottom of the

draw pack. Team B's turn continues until they answer incorrectly or until they have answered five questions in a row correctly.

- The question reader from Team B now draws a question from the pack and reads it to Team A.
- Continue play in this manner for the time you have allotted. At the end of the game, the team with the most questions in their "correct" pile wins.

Trivia Game 2

- Divide the class into equal-sized teams of about three or four students each. Have the teams sit together.
- Each team selects one "panelist" and one "reader." The panelists bring their bibles and sit in front of the rest of the group. Give each panelist some small slips of paper and a pencil.
- You will need one pack of trivia cards. To begin play, the reader from Team 1 draws a question from the pack, and says, for example: "The answer to this question can be found in Mark." Pause while everyone opens to Mark. The reader then continues, "How old was the young girl Jesus brought back to life?" The panelists leaf through their bibles looking for the answer. All the other participants also look for the answer, so they will know if the panelists are right or wrong.
- When the panelists find the answer, they write the scripture reference—Mk 5:42—on their slips of paper and stand. If the panelists are very slow in finding an answer, gradually give them additional clues; for example, "It is early in Mark. It is in chapter 5. It's at the end of the chapter." Note the order when the panelists stand.
- When all the panelists are standing, check their answers. All of the panelists who have correct answers receive points for their teams—the first one standing gets five points, the second gets four points, and so on. Keep track of the points on the board or on a score pad. In case of a tie, award equal points to both panelists.
- The reader from Team 2 now draws a question from the trivia cards to read to the panelists, and so on. (You may also choose to read the questions yourself.)

- When each of the readers has read one or two questions, retire the panel and have each team select a second panelist. Continue with as many rounds as you have time for. No team can send a person up as panelist a second time until everyone on the team has had a turn.
- The team with the most points wins the game.

Beatitude Drills

Beatitudes Individual and Pair Study Drill

- Duplicate the **Beatitude List (page 165)**, one copy for each student.
- Duplicate the **Beatitude Study Cards (pages 167-168)**, putting the first half of the beatitude on the front of the card, the second half on the back. Make one set for each student.
- Distribute the lists. Read each beatitude to the class and have them repeat it after you. Allow a few minutes for the students to study the list quietly, then recite the entire list together.
- Now give each person a set of beatitude study cards, and instruct them to lay out the cards in order, with the "blessed" side up, using the list for a guide.
- Next, tell the students to put away the list and study from the cards, reading the "blessed" side quietly, thinking the "for" side, then turning the card over to see if they thought it correctly.
- After individual study, have the students work in pairs. One person turns all of his or her cards so the "blessed" side is up; the other so that the "for" side is up. Mix up the cards, then work together to put them in proper order. Use the lists to check.
- Repeat the above, only this time after the cards are in mixed-up order ready to be matched, have the teams switch places so they are working on someone else's set of cards. Race to see which team is the first to finish correctly. Use the list to check one another's work. This can be repeated several times.

Beatitudes Large Group Drill

- Make two sets of one-sided **Beatitude Study Cards (page 167-168)**. On one set, put the first half of each beatitude (beginning with "blessed"). On the second set, put the second half of each beatitude (beginning with "for"). For longer wear, run these on card stock or laminate them. You may also want to enlarge these cards so they can be read from a greater distance.
- Spread out the "for" cards on a table in front of the group. Distribute the "blessed" cards face-side down to eight students. When you say GO, the students with cards run to the table, pick out the matching "for" card, and stand in front of the class, arranging themselves in order.
- When all are in order, the students holding the cards lead the class in reciting the beatitudes.
- Repeat the process, distributing the "blessed" cards to another set of eight students.
- If you have at least sixteen students in your class, play this game with two competing teams. Each team will need a separate spread of "for" cards to choose from and of course a separate set of the "blessed" cards as well. The first team to be standing in front in correct order wins the game.

Bible Books Game

- This game is designed for groups of four to six. Determine how many groups you will have and then duplicate the **Bible Books Key Word Cards (pages 169-171)**, making one set for each small group. Put each set in an envelope.
- Duplicate the two **Bible Outline Pages (pages 172-173)**, one set for each small group.
- Divide the class into groups of four to six. Assign each group to a table.
- Give each group the outline pages and a lunch bag containing a set of the Bible books key word cards.
- Instruct the groups to work together to match the names of the books to the proper categories on the outline page. Each person

should draw a key word card and place it in the box of the correct category. Teammates make corrections if needed. When all groups have finished, check the exercise together, then have the tables put the key word cards back into the lunch bag.

- Repeat the matching exercise, this time as a contest between tables. When all are ready call "Go." The first table to finish stands. They win only if they have no errors.
- Instruct the tables to choose two representative who will do the matching game for their team. Have the reps move to another table. They should remain standing to do the exercise. When they have finished, ask the table group to check for errors. The first pair of reps to complete the exercise correctly wins the round. Mark the score on the board.
- Have each table select two new representatives. Assign them to a different table and repeat the matching game.
- Repeat until all have had a chance to be team reps.

Option: You may wish to do this exercise in two parts at first, separating the Old Testament books from the New Testament.

Old Testament Answers

Pentateuch (The Torah)	*Historical Books*
Genesis	Joshua
Exodus	Judges
Leviticus	Ruth
Numbers	1 and 2 Samuel
Deuteronomy	1 and 2 Kings
	1 and 2 Chronicles
	Ezra
	Nehemiah
	Tobit
	Judith
	Esther
	1 and 2 Maccabees

Wisdom Books
Job

Psalms

Proverbs

Ecclesiastes

Song of Songs

Wisdom

Sirach

Prophetic Books
Isaiah

Jeremiah

Lamentations

Baruch

Ezekiel

Daniel

Hosea

Joel

Amos

Obadiah

Jonah

Micah

Nahum

Habakkuk

Zephaniah

Haggai

Zechariah

Malachi

New Testament Answers
Gospels
Matthew

Mark

Luke

John

History of Early Christian Church
Acts of the Apostles

Letters by Paul
Romans

1 and 2 Corinthians

Galatians

Ephesians

Philippians

Colossians

1 and 2 Thessalonians

1 and 2 Timothy

Titus

Other Letters
Philemon

James

1 and 2 Peter

1, 2, and 3 John

Jude

Hebrews

Revelation to John

Sacraments Word Search

- Duplicate the **Sacraments Word Search (page 174)**, making one copy for each small group.
- Explain that the grid contains at least forty words related to the celebration of sacraments. (The word search is modeled on the game Boggle®.) The letters of the words might be found down, up, across, or diagonal and can change direction within the word, but each letter must touch the letter before, and no letter can be used more than once in one word.
- Instruct the group to work together as a team searching for the words. Assign a recorder to make a list of all the words found. To count, a word must be related to the sacraments in some way and be at least four letters long.
- Allow time for the groups to find many of the words. Then tell each group to send their recorder to another table for checking. One point is awarded for each word found, and minus one point for any word listed that is not on the grid. (Be prepared to arbitrate here; the students will have some interesting ways of relating words to the sacraments. Your judgment as to whether a given word counts is final.)

Option: Give everyone a copy of the grid to take home and continue searching for the missing words.

List of Possible Words

Absolution • Anointing of the Sick • Baptism(s) • Bishop • Bread • Catholic(s) • Chrism • Christ • Church(es) • Commitment • Communion • Confess • Confirmation • Contrition • Creed • Deacon • Faith • Forgiveness • Grace(s) • Holy Eucharist • Holy Orders • Host(s) • Jesus • Mass • Matrimony • Penance • Pray • Prayer(s) • Priest • Reconciliation • Sacrament(s) • Satan • Soul • Sponsor • Touch • Viaticum • Water • Wine

Credo Game

- Credo is the Latin word for "I believe." The Credo game is played like bingo. To begin, select fifty **Study Cards (pages 43-122)** that you want your students to review. You will need cards that have one word or short phrase answers. Mark ten of the cards with C, ten with R, ten with E, ten with D, and ten with O.

- Type the answers from your fifty cards in five columns, putting ten under C, ten under R, etc. Duplicate these answer lists, making one copy for each student and one copy for yourself. See the sample answer list on page 36.

- Duplicate one copy of the **Credo Game Card (page 175)** for each student.

- Give each student a copy of the answer list and the Credo game card. Have them work with a partner to fill in the game card with words from the list. Tell the students they will *not* be playing the game from the cards they make. One of the partners should use any five words (four for "E" column) from each list, printing their words in random order under the letters indicated. The other partner should do the same with the remaining five words. As they work, they should review together any words from the list they might not be sure of.

- Collect the completed Credo game cards and redistribute them randomly to the students.

- To play, you will need an answer list and a bag containing all fifty study cards. As caller, pick a card from the bag and say, "This answer will be found under the C. What word means 'the first four books of the New Testament which tell about the life and teachings of Jesus'? If you find the answer on your game card, circle it." The caller circles the word on the answer list.

- Follow the usual bingo ways of winning the game: across, down, diagonal, four corners. When someone calls "Credo," check by having the winner read the words back to you, giving an explanation of each. Give the winner a small prize (a round of applause will suffice), then continue playing. You can play as long as you have time or until someone has covered his or her entire card.

Catechism Categories Game

C	R	E	D	O
act of contrition	Abba	Creator	Aramic	Ash Wednesday
Beatitudes	Emmanuel	consecration	baptismal font	All Saints' Day
gospels	Golden Rule	disciple	catholic(c)	apostles
Holy Orders	Good Shepherd	fast	chalice	Bible
host	Holy Thursday	forgiveness	Christmas	Cana
John the Baptist	Pope	heaven	Incarnation	Hebrews
marraiage	Resurrection	sacraments	parable	Lent
Mass	Sacred Heart	Sunday obligation	priests	Moses
original sin	sin		sacraments of initiation	Nazareth
Pontius Pilate	Vatican		venial sin	paschal candle

Catechism Categories Game

- Make a Catechism category board like the one below:

Old Testament	New Testament	Sacraments	Creed	Apostles
10	10	10	10	10
20	20	20	20	20
30	30	30	30	30
40	40	40	40	40
50	50	50	50	50

—Post a piece of heavy poster board about 30 inches square so that all can see.

—Prepare five 3″ x 6″ category cards made of card stock or tag board. Print one category (e.g., sacraments) on each card.

—Prepare twenty-five 3″ by 3″ number cards, writing "10 points" on five cards, "20 points" on another five, and so on making 30, 40, and 50 point cards as well. Use card stock or tag board.

—Attach the category cards and numbers to the Catechism category board by putting a small tab of masking tape on the back of each card.

—Prepare a set of twenty-five total questions, five questions for each of the five categories you have chosen. The five questions in each category should be progressively more difficult. (A sample set of questions and answers is listed below. You may also wish to write other questions for these categories, or create your own categories and questions.)

• Divide the class into teams of three or four players each. Instruct the teams to sit together. Draw lots or have team representatives guess a designated number between 1 and 10 to determine which team will be first, second, third, etc.

• To begin play, Team A selects a category and a point value. You read the question they choose. The team confers, then gives you their answer. If they are correct, hand them the point card to keep as a tally. If they are wrong, say the correct answer and remove the point card from the board.

• Team B now selects a category and point value, etc., until all point cards have been removed from the board.

• The team with the highest total point value wins the game.

Sample Questions and Answers

Old Testament

1. Name the first book in the Old Testament. (Genesis)

2. Name the person who is called the Father of the Jewish people. (Abraham)

3. Name the young man who was sold into slavery by his brothers. (Joseph)

4. What do we call a person who "speaks for God"? (prophet)

5. Name five kinds of books that can be found in the Old Testament. (e.g., law, history, wisdom, prophecy, psalms)

New Testament

1. Name the four gospel writers. (Matthew, Mark, Luke, John)

2. Who wrote most of the epistles? (St. Paul)

3. Name two of the Christian groups to whom Paul wrote letters. (e.g., Romans, Corinthians, Galatians, Ephesians, Philippians, Colossians, Thessalonians)

4. Name two books in the New Testament that begin with the letter R. (Romans, Revelation)

5. In what two gospels can we find the Christmas story? (Matthew, Luke)

Sacraments

1. Which sacrament uses the pouring of water to symbolize God's presence? (baptism)

2. Name the seven sacraments. (baptism, confirmation, eucharist, reconciliation, anointing of the sick, marriage, holy orders)

3. Name the three sacraments of initiation. (baptism, confirmation, eucharist)

4. Four sacraments use oil in the celebration. Name three of them. (e.g., baptism, confirmation, anointing of the sick, holy orders)

5. There are three different stages or levels of holy orders. Name two of them. (e.g., diaconate, presbyterate, episcopacy or deacon, priest, bishop)

Creed

1. What phrase in the creed describes what happened on Easter Sunday? (he rose from the dead)

2. Who was the Roman governor when Jesus was condemned? (Pilate)

3. What phrase in the creed tells about our connection to the holy people in heaven and the suffering souls in purgatory? (communion of saints)

4. What word in the creed reminds us that our church is for all people? (catholic)

5. What words in the creed tell us that Joseph was not the human father of Jesus? (conceived by the Holy Spirit)

Apostles

1. Who did Jesus appoint to be the leader of the apostles? (Simon Peter)

2. Which apostle betrayed Jesus? (Judas)

3. Name two apostles who were brothers. (e.g., Peter and Andrew, or James and John)

4. Which apostle had been a tax collector before he started following Jesus? (Levi/Matthew)

5. Who was chosen to take Judas's place after the resurrection? (Matthias)

Team Toss

Note: This game can be used as a large group review or to drill questions that have multiple part answers; e.g., those involving the sacraments, gifts of the Holy Spirit, twelve apostles. It also works to drill words or phrases from a prayer.

• Select the lists or prayers that are to be reviewed. Distribute copies to everyone in the class and allow a few minutes to review together.

• Procure a ball that can be easily tossed back and forth, preferably a sponge ball that won't roll away when dropped. (A pair of rolled up socks or mittens can also be used.)

• Divide the class into two equal teams. Have the teams sit in two rows, about four feet apart, facing one another. (They can sit in chairs or on the floor.)

• Call out the category or prayer that is being reviewed, e.g., sacraments. Toss the ball to one of the students on Team A. He or she calls out the name of one of the sacraments, and tosses the ball to someone on Team B. The person who catches the ball calls out another sacrament, and tosses the ball to a different person on Team A. Continue until the list is completed, or until someone misses.

- A miss occurs when a player:
    —doesn't know another item from the list (or the next word or phrase from the prayer)

    —hesitates more than three seconds

    —gives an item that is not on the list

    —gives an item that has already been called

    —is prompted by someone else on the team.

    When the miss occurs, the teacher retrieves the ball.

- If the list is completed without a miss on either team, both teams get a score equal to the number of items in the list. When a miss is called, the team that didn't miss gets a score equal to the number of items that were given before the miss. The game then continues, with one point given for each correct answer.

- For a second round, call out another category or prayer, and toss the ball to someone on Team B.

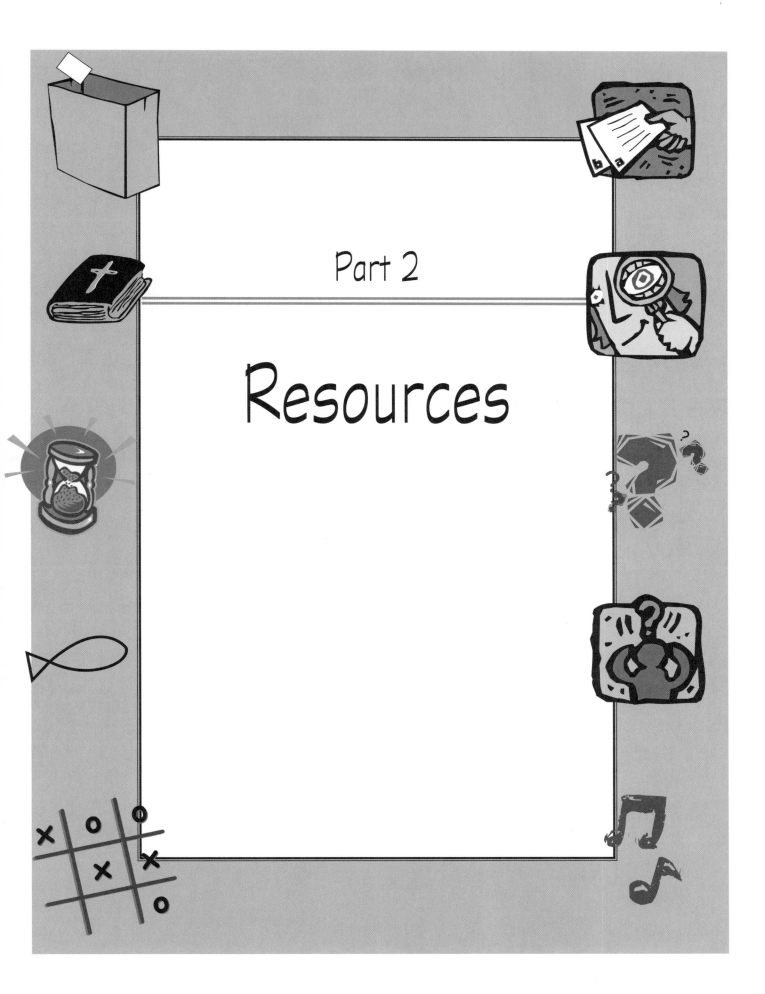

Part 2

Resources

1. Abraham	2. act of contrition
3. Adam and Eve	4. Advent
5. Advent wreath	6. altar
7. Amen	8. angels
9. anointing of the sick	10. apostles

2. A prayer we say to tell God that we are sorry for our sins.	**1.** The spiritual father of the Jewish people.
4. The Church season that prepares for the coming of Christ at Christmas.	**3.** The first humans created by God. They lived in the Garden of Eden.
6. The holy table on which the sacrifice of the Mass is offered.	**5.** An evergreen wreath in which four candles are set. One additional candle is lit on each Sunday of Advent.
8. Spiritual beings with intelligence and free will who act as messengers for God.	**7.** The word means "Yes! Let it be so!" When you say or sing this word, it means you agree with what has been said.
10. The twelve leaders Jesus chose and sent forth to continue the work he began.	**9.** The sacrament of healing which is celebrated when one is in danger of death or has an extended or serious illness.

11. Apostles' Creed	**12. archbishop**
13. baptism	**14. Bethlehem**
15. Bible	**16. bishop**
17. Blessed Mother	**18. Blessed Sacrament**
19. Calvary (Golgotha)	**20. Cana**

12. A bishop of the highest rank; the head of a major Church territory known as an archdiocese.	**11. One of the earliest creeds of the Church. It summarizes the faith of the early Christians and our faith.**
14. The town in Judea where Jesus was born.	**13. The sacrament by which we become members of the Church and adopted children of God.**
16. A successor of the apostles; the leader of a diocese.	**15. The book that contains the written word of God for Christians.**
18. The bread which was consecrated at Mass, reserved in the tabernacle.	**17. Another name for Mary. She is called this because she is the Mother of Jesus and our mother, too.**
20. The place where Jesus performed his first miracle by changing water into wine.	**19. The name of the hill on which Jesus was crucified.**

21. Catholic (uppercase "C")	22. catholic (lowercase "c")
23. Christ	24. Christians
25. Christmas	26. church (lowercase c)
27. commandments	28. confirmation
29. creation	30. Creator

22. A word that means "universal" or "for everyone."

21. The name of a major Christian religion. Its people follow the pope as their leader and celebrate the seven sacraments.

24. People who are baptized and believe in Jesus Christ.

23. The Greek word for "Messiah" or "Chosen One." It is the most important title given to Jesus by the Church.

26. A gathering of people who come together to worship God; the building in which people who come together to worship God gather.

25. The season of the Church year that celebrates the Son of God becoming man; the birthday of Jesus.

28. The sacrament that completes baptism and celebrates the special gifts of the Holy Spirit.

27. Laws given by God to his people as a sign of his covenant with them; they list our responsibilities to God and to our neighbor.

30. The title we use for God as the maker of heaven, earth, and all things.

29. People, animals, and nature—everything made by God.

31. crucifix	32. diocese
33. Easter	34. Eucharist
35. forgiveness	36. God the Father
37. God the Holy Spirit	38. God the Son
39. godparent	40. Golden Rule

32. A geographical region of the Church under the leadership of a local bishop.

31. A cross with a figure of Christ on it.

34. The sacrament of Jesus' presence under the appearances of bread and wine. The word means "thanksgiving."

33. The season of the Church Year that celebrates the resurrection of Jesus.

36. God as Creator and origin of all things, to whom all creation owes worship and glory; the first Person of the Holy Trinity.

35. A gift God offers us when we have sinned and expects us to offer those who offend us.

38. God who became a human being, lived on earth, died for our sins, and rose from the dead; the second Person of the Holy Trinity.

37. God's own love and holiness present within the Church, guiding and directing God's people; the third Person of the Holy Trinity.

40. "Do unto others whatever you would have them do unto you."

39. A person who acts as a sponsor to someone who is baptized.

41. Good Friday	**42. grace at meals**
43. Great Commandment	**44. Hail Mary**
45. heaven	**46. hell**
47. Holy Communion	**48. Holy Family**
49. Holy Land	**50. holy orders**

42. A prayer or blessing that people share before eating, asking God to bless both the food and those who are about to share it.

41. The day the Church remembers that Jesus died on the cross for love of us.

44. A prayer that honors Mary. It begins with the words of the angel Gabriel when he greeted Mary at the Annunciation.

43. The commandment to love God, others, and self. It was revealed to the people of the Old Covenant and renewed by Jesus Christ in the New Covenant.

46. Being separated from God and God's love forever.

45. Being with God forever. Not a place but a state of being filled with complete and unending joy.

48. Jesus, Mary, and Joseph living together in their home in Nazareth.

47. Receiving the Body and Blood of Christ under the appearances of bread and wine.

50. The sacrament in which men are consecrated to serve God and the Church as bishops, priests, and deacons.

49. The land where Jesus lived; the country of Palestine.

51. Holy Thursday	**52. Holy Trinity**
53. holy water	**54. Holy Week**
55. host	**56. image of God**
57. Jerusalem	**58. Jesus Christ**
59. John Paul II	**60. John the Baptist**

52. The mystery that teaches that the one God is revealed to us as three distinct Persons— God the Father, God the Son, and God the Holy Spirit.

51. The remembrance of the night that Jesus celebrated the Last Supper with his disciples.

54. The week of the liturgical year that begins with Palm Sunday and ends with Easter.

53. Water which has been blessed by a priest. It is used by Christians to remind them of their baptism.

56. The term used in the Bible to tell us that God created us and that we share in God's own life.

55. A small piece of bread used for the celebration of the Eucharist. After it is blessed at Mass it is the Body of Christ.

58. The Son of God, who became man, preached about the kingdom of God, was crucified, and rose from the dead.

57. The main city in ancient Palestine; the center of Jewish religious and political activity at the time of Jesus.

60. The cousin of Jesus and the son of Elizabeth. He baptized Jesus in the River Jordan.

59. Born Karol Wojtyla, he became the first Polish pope in 1978.

Study Cards, Set A

61. Joseph (New Testament)	**62. Joseph (Old Testament)**
63. Last Supper	**64. Law of Love**
65. Lent	**66. Lord's Day**
67. Lord's Prayer	**68. Lord's Supper**
69. Magi	**70. manger**

62. This young man was sold into slavery by his brothers; later he became a great leader of the Hebrew people.

61. The man who was the husband of Mary and foster father of Jesus; he was a carpenter.

64. The "great commandment" given to us by Jesus: to love God with all our hearts, and to love one another as much as he loves us.

63. The meal Jesus and his disciples ate together before he died; at this meal Jesus instituted the Eucharist and gave us the gift of his Body and Blood.

66. Sunday; the day on which Christians celebrate the resurrection of Jesus.

65. The season of the Church year that helps us prepare for Easter. It begins with Ash Wednesday and is commemorated over forty days.

68. The name the early Christians gave to the Eucharist.

67. The Our Father; the prayer that Jesus himself taught us.

70. A feeding box for farm animals. Jesus was laid in one of these when he was born in the stable in Bethlehem.

69. The wise men who came from the East to acknowledge Jesus as a king. Their visit is remembered on the feast of the Epiphany.

71. Mary	**72. Mass**
73. Matrimony	**74. miracle**
75. Nativity	**76. Nazareth**
77. neighbor	**78. New Testament**
79. Noah	**80. Old Testament**

72. A celebration at which Catholics gather to listen to God's word, praise and thank God, and receive communion.	**71.** The mother of Jesus; the Mother of God; the mother of the Church.
74. A wonderful event which shows God's power and love. Jesus performed many of these to show people he had been sent by God.	**73.** The sacrament that unites a baptized man and woman in a lifelong bond of faithful love.
76. The small town where Jesus lived with his parents and where he first preached in its synagogues.	**75.** The name (besides Christmas) for the feast that celebrates the birth of Jesus.
78. The second main part of the Bible; it contains the writings of the apostles and early Christians.	**77.** A fellow human being; a person who lives close to us. Jesus wants us to treat everyone like this, especially people in need.
80. The first part of the Bible; it contains the writings of the Hebrew prophets and the history of the Jewish people.	**79.** A man called by God to build an ark in order to save his family and all the animals from a great flood.

81. parable	82. parish
83. Peter	84. pope
85. prayer	86. priests
87. reconciliation	88. religion
89. rosary	90. sacraments

82. The Church community in a town or neighborhood.	81. A special kind of teaching story, often with a surprise ending, used by Jesus to tell us about the kingdom of God.
84. The leader of the whole Catholic Church; the successor of St. Peter.	83. The man chosen by Jesus to be the head of his Church and the leader of the apostles; the first pope.
86. Men chosen and consecrated in the sacrament of holy orders to celebrate Eucharist and the other sacraments with God's people.	85. Talking and listening to God, using one's own words or reciting formal rituals.
88. A system of beliefs, values, rituals, and other practices based upon the love of God and/or the ideas of a spiritual leader.	87. The sacrament (also known as penance) that celebrates God's forgiveness and reunites us with God and with the Church. The word means "making peace."
90. Seven signs of God's love and sources of God's grace, given by Jesus to his Church. They allow us to share in the life of God.	89. A prayer which honors Mary and remembers the special events in the life of Jesus and Mary; the beads on which this prayer is said.

91. Sacred Heart	**92. saints**
93. Satan	**94. Savior**
95. Scripture	**96. sign of peace**
97. Sign of the Cross	**98. sin**
99. soul	**100. stealing**

92. Holy people recognized and honored by the Church as now living in eternal happiness with God.

91. A devotion to Jesus that focuses on his heart as a symbol of his great love for all people.

94. The title we give to Jesus because he saves us from sin and death.

93. The prince of devils; a fallen angel.

96. A handshake, hug, or kiss shared at Holy Mass to remind us that Jesus calls us to love our neighbors.

95. The writings inspired by the Holy Spirit that have been collected in the Bible. The word itself means "writings."

98. A word, deed, or desire contrary to the will of God; an offense against God.

97. A prayer in honor of the Blessed Trinity, said while tracing the shape of a cross on our bodies.

100. The taking of what belongs to another without permission.

99. The spiritual nature of humans; it is the part of us which will never die.

1. Abba	2. abortion
3. absolution	4. adoration
5. All Saints' Day	6. All Soul's Day
7. Alleluia	8. Annunciation, feast of the
9. anoint	10. Aramaic

2. The grave sin of deliberately causing the death of an unborn child.

1. The name Jesus used when he talked to God in prayer. It is the Aramaic word for "Daddy."

4. The highest form of praise given only to God.

3. The words of forgiveness prayed by the priest in the sacrament of reconciliation.

6. The feast on November 2 when the Church remembers and prays for all the people who have died.

5. The Church feast on November 1 that honors all the people in heaven, especially those who have not been canonized.

8. The March 25 feast day that celebrates the angel announcing to Mary that she was chosen to be the Mother of Jesus.

7. A Hebrew expression that means "praise God."

10. The language Jesus spoke when he was on earth. Some of the books of the Bible were first written in this language.

9. To rub with blessed oil.

11. Ascension, feast of the	**12. Ash Wednesday**
13. Assumption, feast of the	**14. Baptism of Jesus**
15. baptismal font	**16. Beatitudes**
17. blessings	**18. Body of Christ**
19. canonization	**20. chalice**

12. The first day of Lent. Christians are signed with ashes made from burned palms as a call to turn away from sin and come back to God.

11. The return of Jesus, body and soul, to his Father in heaven. The feast is celebrated forty days after Easter.

14. During this event, which happened in the River Jordan, a voice from heaven proclaimed that Jesus is God's Son.

13. The August 15 feast that celebrates our belief that Mary was taken into heaven body and soul when she died.

16. The gospel values taught by Jesus at the Sermon on the Mount naming the true happiness with which God blesses his people.

15. A special place in the Church where baptisms are celebrated.

18. This phrase names both the consecrated bread and the people who believe in Jesus and follow his teachings.

17. Prayers of praise and thanksgiving that remember God's presence with us.

20. A cup used to hold the consecrated wine at Eucharist.

19. The process by which the Church declares a person to be a saint.

21. chapel	22. charity
23. choir	24. confession
25. consecration	26. contrition
27. creeds	28. deacons
29. Decalogue	30. disciple

22. The theological virtue which helps us love God and others as they wish to be loved, unselfishly and without condition.

21. A place of worship and prayer that is smaller than a church; it is usually found in buildings like hospitals and schools.

24. The act of telling our sins to the priest in the sacrament of reconciliation; also another name for the sacrament.

23. A group of people who sing together.

26. True sorrow for sin and the firm intention of not sinning again.

25. The solemn prayer during the Mass when the bread and wine are changed into the Body and Blood of Christ.

28. Men consecrated in the sacrament of holy orders to assist bishops and priests, especially in the ministry of mercy and charity.

27. Prayers that contain a summary of what the Church believes and teaches.

30. One who is a follower and a learner; someone who helps in spreading the teachings and values of another.

29. A name for the Ten Commandments which literally means "ten words."

31. dove	**32. Easter Triduum**
33. Easter Vigil	**34. Ecumenical Council**
35. Emmanuel	**36. Epistles**
37. eucharistic prayer	**38. examination of conscience**
39. faith	**40. fast**

32. The three great holy days of Holy Thursday, Good Friday, and the Easter Vigil.

31. A symbol for the Holy Spirit. Also, used as a symbol for peace.

34. A gathering of all bishops of the world in order to make solemn decisions for the whole Church.

33. The liturgical celebration that takes place on Holy Saturday night. It includes blessing the new fire, readings and songs, and the sacraments of initiation.

36. The letters in the New Testament, written by Paul and other disciples. The word comes from the Greek word for "letter."

35. One of the names given to Jesus in the Bible; it means "God is with us."

38. Taking time to think about our choices and actions to see if they have been in keeping with God's will for us.

37. During Mass, the great prayer of thanksgiving. It culminates in the words of consecration.

40. To go without food for a period of time as a sign of our love for God and as a way of doing penance for our sins.

39. The gift given by God that moves us to believe in him and in his revelation. It is one of the theological virtues.

41. free will	**42. Gabriel**
43. Gethsemane	**44. Good Samaritan**
45. Good Shepherd	**46. gospels**
47. grace	**48. Guadalupe**
49. Hebrew Scriptures	**50. Hebrews**

42. The angel who announced to Mary that she would be the Mother of God.

41. The gift of God which allows human beings to choose between good and evil and to freely accept or reject the love of God.

44. A story told by Jesus about a good person who stopped to help a stranger in need.

43. The name of the garden where Jesus prayed the night before he was crucified.

46. The first four books of the New Testament; they tell about the life and teachings of Jesus.

45. A title given to Jesus that shows his loving protection, and his willingness to come looking for us when we go astray.

48. The place in Mexico where the Virgin Mary appeared to a peasant named Juan Diego.

47. A share in God's own life and love within us. God's free, unlimited, loving gift of himself to us human beings.

50. Another name for the Jews, God's Chosen People.

49. The Jewish sacred writings, which contain the story of God's loving relationship with Israel. Christians call these writings the Old Testament.

51. holiness	**52. homily**
53. hope	**54. hymn**
55. Incarnation	**56. Jews**
57. John	**58. kingdom of God**
59. laity	**60. marriage**

52. A talk given by a priest or deacon at Mass to help us understand the scripture readings and apply them to our lives.

51. Living in close union with God. God's presence to us and our loving fidelity to God.

54. A song of praise to God that we sing at church and at home.

53. The theological virtue that helps us to trust in God and God's promises above everyone and everything else.

56. Descendants from the Israelites, also called Hebrews. Jesus belonged to this people.

55. The mystery which states that Jesus is both God and man; that the Son of God "took on flesh," and became a human being.

58. A name for God's power and love working in the world. Jesus came to proclaim this, and to invite all people to belong.

57. This apostle was known as the "beloved disciple." He is also one of the four evangelists.

60. The legal union of a man and a woman as husband and wife.

59. All the members of the Church who have not been ordained in the sacrament of holy orders.

61. minister	**62. ministry**
63. monks	**64. mortal sin**
65. Moses	**66. Mother Teresa of Calcutta**
67. nuns	**68. ordination**
69. original sin	**70. paschal candle**

62. Loving service to others, part of the baptismal call of every Christian.

61. A person who serves others in one of many ways—for example, by reading God's word, giving communion, visiting the sick.

64. A very serious offense that destroys our relationship with God.

63. Men who take religious vows and live a communal life of quiet prayer and work within a monastery.

66. A twentieth century nun who cared for dying persons with no place to go and who founded an order of sisters to continue her work.

65. A great leader of the Hebrew people. He led his people out of the slavery of Egypt into the Promised Land. His name means "drawn from water."

68. To invest a person with Church authority through the sacrament of holy orders.

67. Religious women who dedicate their lives to God and the service of God's people. They take vows of poverty, chastity, and obedience.

70. The symbol of the Risen Christ that stands in the sanctuary from Easter to Ascension.

69. The separation from God that has been part of all human lives since people first turned away from God.

71. passion of Jesus	**72. pastor**
73. penance	**74. Pentecost**
75. Pontius Pilate	**76. Prodigal Son**
77. Promised Land	**78. prophet**
79. reconciliation room	**80. Resurrection**

72. The priest who leads a parish community.	**71.** The story of Jesus' suffering and death as told by the writers of the gospels.
74. A word that means "fiftieth day." It is the feast celebrated fifty days after Easter that remembers the coming of the Holy Spirit on the Church.	**73.** A way to make up for our sins and to practice making better choices; a prayer assigned by the priest in the sacrament of reconciliation.
76. The parable Jesus tells about a young man who wasted his father's inheritance but was lovingly forgiven when he returned home.	**75.** The Roman governor of Palestine at the time of the trial and death of Jesus.
78. A word that describes a person "who speaks for God."	**77.** The biblical name for Canaan, the land God promised to the children of Abraham and Sarah.
80. The mystery of Jesus being raised from the dead by God's loving power. This mystery celebrated on Easter Sunday.	**79.** A place in the church to celebrate the sacrament of forgiveness.

81. Rome	82. Sabbath
83. sacramentals	84. sacraments of healing
85. sacraments of initiation	86. sacraments of service
87. sacrifice	88. sanctuary
89. Sea of Galilee	90. seal of confession

82. The weekly day of rest and worship; celebrated on Saturday by Jews and Sunday by Christians.

81. The city where the apostles Peter and Paul died; the place where Vatican City is.

84. reconciliation (penance) and anointing of the sick.

83. Objects, actions, and blessings of the Church that remind us of God's presence and strengthen our faith in God.

86. holy orders and matrimony.

85. baptism, confirmation, and Eucharist.

88. The main area in the church building where the altar is placed.

87. Something precious offered to God out of love and worship; something difficult given or done for another's good.

90. The absolute confidentiality required of a priest regarding sins revealed to him in confession.

89. A lake located in the Holy Land where the apostles fished and where several miracles of Jesus took place.

91. Second Vatican Council	**92. seminary**
93. Sermon on the Mount	**94. sponsor**
95. Sunday obligation	**96. tabernacle**
97. temptation	**98. unleavened bread**
99. Vatican City	**100. venial sin**

92. A school which trains people to be priests or other ministers.

91. A meeting of all the bishops from around the world which was held in Rome from 1962 to 1965.

94. One who helps another live according to the responsibilities of Christian life; this person often accompanies another at Confirmation.

93. Several teachings of Jesus grouped together in Matthew 5 which describe the actions and attitudes of true disciples in response to the love of God.

96. The special locked cabinet, often made of gold, where the Blessed Sacrament is kept in a Catholic church.

95. The expectation that Catholics are to participate in the Eucharist every Sunday and holy day.

98. Bread baked without yeast so that it does not rise; it is used by Jewish people for Passover and by Catholics for Eucharist.

97. An invitation or desire to do something we know we are not supposed to do.

100. Sin that weakens but does not destroy our covenant with God or our relationship with others.

99. The small city, located within the city of Rome, which is the headquarters of the Catholic Church and the home of the pope.

1. actual grace	2. Advocate
3. alb	4. almsgiving
5. ambo	6. Angelus
7. Antioch	8. apostolic
9. apostolic succession	10. Ark of the Covenant

2. A title of the Holy Spirit which means helper. Jesus promised to send the Holy Spirit to help the church remember and understand his teachings.

1. The help we receive every day from God to live our lives as children of God.

4. The free giving of food, money, and clothing to the poor.

3. The long white robe worn by priests or deacons when they lead a public prayer.

6. A prayer that was traditionally repeated three times a day—at morning, noon, and evening—with the ringing of church bells.

5. The special podium in the church where the word of God is proclaimed.

8. One of the four marks of the Church. It shows that the Church is founded on and faithful to the teachings of the apostles.

7. A city which was the home of a very early Christian community. Here the followers of Jesus were first called "Christians."

10. A special container in which the Israelites kept the stone tablets of the Law.

9. The unbroken chain of authority that extends from the apostles to the bishops of today.

11. canon law	12. catechesis
13. catechist	14. catechumen
15. cathedral	16. celibacy
17. chasuble	18. chrism
19. chrismation	20. Christian Initiation

12. The teaching of the faith; the passing on of the truths of Christianity	**11.** The basic set of regulations that govern the life of the Catholic Church, from celebrating the sacraments to electing the pope.
14. A person receiving instruction in the fundamentals of Christianity in preparation for baptism.	**13.** Someone who teaches others about God and God's word.
16. A promise to God not to marry or to engage in any sexual activity.	**15.** The official church of the diocese; a place where the bishop resides.
18. The oil used in the sacraments of baptism, confirmation, and holy orders; it is consecrated by the bishop on Holy Thursday.	**17.** A garment worn by the priest at Mass. The color (white, green, red, or purple) fits the season or feast day being celebrated.
20. The process by which a person becomes a member of the Church; it includes the sacraments of baptism, confirmation, and Eucharist.	**19.** The name used for confirmation in Eastern churches.

21. college of bishops	**22. communion of saints**
23. conscience	**24. covenant**
25. covet	**26. divine providence**
27. Epiphany, feast of the	**28. evangelists**
29. Exodus	**30. Genesis**

22. All the followers of Jesus, living and dead, including the faithful on earth, the souls in purgatory, and the saints in heaven.

21. All the Catholic bishops of the world, in union with their head, the Pope, who is the bishop of Rome.

24. A sacred and binding agreement between God and his people.

23. The inner truth by which we know the difference between right and wrong.

26. God's loving and faithful care for his people; especially his way of taking care of our needs.

25. To desire something which rightly belongs to someone else.

28. The name used for the four authors of the gospels; it means "bearer of good news."

27. The feast which recalls the visit of the magi to the Child Jesus; the word means "manifestation."

30. The name of the first book of the Bible that tells the origins of God's People; the word means "beginning" or "origins."

29. The passage of the Israelites from slavery in Egypt to freedom in the Promised Land. Also the name of the second book in the Old Testament.

31. gentiles	32. genuflect
33. holy	34. holy days of obligation
35. hosanna	36. Immaculate Conception, feast of the
37. immersion	38. INRI
39. Isaac	40. Israelites

32. A sign of respect—touching our right knee to the floor—we show when we enter and leave the presence of Jesus in church.

31. The name Jewish people use to refer to people who are not Jewish.

34. Days other than Sundays on which faithful Catholics are obliged to attend Mass.

33. One of the four marks of the Church; it shows that the Church comes from God and shows people the way to God. God is the ultimate source of this mark.

36. The feast the celebrates the belief that Mary was free from all sin, including original sin, from the first moment of her life.

35. This Hebrew word means "praise be to God." The people shouted this and waved palms as Jesus rode into Jerusalem on a donkey.

38. Letters that stand for "Jesus of Nazareth, King of the Jews." These words were hung on the cross over Jesus' head.

37. A form of baptism in which the baptized person is completely covered by water while the words "I baptize you . . ." are being said.

40. A name used for the descendants of Abraham, the people God chose as his own; also known as Jews.

39. The son of Abraham and Sarah. He was about to be sacrificed by his father but was saved by a message from God.

41. Joshua	**42. Jude**
43. last rites	**44. lector**
45. litany	**46. liturgical year**
47. Liturgy of the Eucharist	**48. Liturgy of the Word**
49. Luther	**50. manna**

42. The patron saint of "lost causes."

41. The successor of Moses as leader of the Israelites.

44. A liturgical minister who proclaims God's word at Mass or in liturgical settings. The word means "reader."

43. The rituals celebrated by Catholics at the time of death. They include the sacrament of anointing of the sick, the sacrament of reconciliation, and reception of communion.

46. The cycle of seasons and feasts that make up the Church's year of worship and celebrate God's saving plan of love.

45. A form of prayer that is made up of a long list of invocations and responses.

48. The part of the Mass that is made up of readings from the Old Testament, the epistles, and the gospels, as well as the homily.

47. The second main part of the Mass, including the great prayer of thanksgiving, the consecration, the Lord's Prayer, and communion.

50. The bread-like substance with which God fed the Israelites in the desert.

49. A German priest who set out to reform abuses in the Church, but ended up breaking relations with the Catholic Church; this break marks the beginning of the Protestant Reformation.

51. Mary Magdalene	**52. mercy**
53. Messiah	**54. Michael the Archangel**
55. missionary	**56. miter**
57. monastery	**58. morality**
59. myth	**60. Nicene Creed**

52. The attribute of God that names his always faithful love, his concern for our good, and his willingness to forgive us.	**51. One of the women who followed Jesus; she was the first person to whom he appeared after his resurrection.**
54. The archangel described in the book of Revelation as fighting for good over evil.	**53. A Hebrew title of Jesus which means "anointed one."**
56. The name for the pointed hat worn by the bishop.	**55. A person who is sent to share the gospel with others, especially in a foreign country.**
58. A name to describe a set of ideals which guide right behavior; a set of teachings that guide the choices we make.	**57. A home for a religious community of men called monks.**
60. A prayer said at Mass professing what Christians believe. It was written at the Council of Nicea (325 AD) and modified at the Council of Constantinople (381 AD).	**59. A story or poem that deals with the mysteries of life and attempts to explain life's inner meaning and purpose.**

61. Our Lady of Guadalupe	**62. Palm Sunday**
63. Passover	**64. Paul**
65. Pentateuch	**66. People of God**
67. permanent deacons	**68. pilgrimage**
69. Pope John XXIII	**70. rectory**

62. The Sunday before Easter; also known as Passion Sunday. We carry blessed branches in procession on this day.

61. A title given to Mary who appeared in Mexico to a peasant named Juan Diego. We celebrate the feast on December 12.

64. This person was known as Saul before he became a Christian. He is the author of most of the epistles in the New Testament.

63. A seven-day Jewish festival that recalls the escape of the Hebrew people from Egypt.

66. A name used to describe the Church as the people chosen by God to be his special family and to spread his love to all nations.

65. The Greek name given to the first five books of the Old Testament; the Jewish people call these books the Torah.

68. A religious journey to a sacred place.

67. Men consecrated in the sacrament of holy orders to assist bishops and priests, especially in the ministry of mercy and charity, who will serve in this role for their lifetime. They may be married when they are ordained.

70. The house on the parish property in which the priest lives.

69. The pope who called the Second Vatican Council. He said he wanted to "open the windows" of the Church to let in the "fresh air" of the Holy Spirit.

Study Cards, Set C

71. Redeemer	**72. reverence**
73. rites	**74. ritual**
75. sanctifying grace	**76. server**
77. sexuality	**78. shroud of Turin**
79. St. Francis of Assisi	**80. St. Jerome**

72. The deep honor and respect we owe to God, and to all that God has made.

71. A title for Jesus based on a word that means "buy back" or "ransom." Jesus suffered and died to "buy us back" from the power of sin.

74. A formal religious ceremony that proceeds according to set rules.

73. Prayers and symbolic actions used in the celebration of the liturgy.

76. One who helps the celebrant during the celebration of Mass or another sacrament.

75. The gift of God's life and love acting within our hearts to make us holy.

78. A relic believed by Christians to be the cloth in which Christ's body was wrapped at his burial. The image of his body can be seen on the cloth.

77. The physical, psychological, and spiritual characteristics that differentiate males and females.

80. A fifth century scripture scholar who translated the Bible from Greek, Hebrew, and Aramaic into Latin, which was then the common language of the people.

79. An Italian saint who embraced poverty and is known for his love of animals.

81. Stations of the Cross	82. stole
83. suicide	84. symbol
85. synagogue	86. theology
87. Thomas	88. Tradition (uppercase T)
89. tradition (lowercase t)	90. transubstantiation

82. A narrow strip of cloth (something like a scarf) worn by bishops, priests, and deacons during liturgical rituals.	**81.** A Catholic devotion that walks the journey to Calvary with Jesus, stopping to pray at fourteen pictures depicting something that happened to Jesus.
84. A thing or action used to express a hidden or invisible reality.	**83.** The direct taking of one's own life.
86. This word means "the study of God."	**85.** The house of worship and community center for Jewish people.
88. The collected teachings and practices of the Church that are not written in the scriptures.	**87.** An apostle whose name means "twin"; he is called "the doubter" because he wouldn't believe Jesus had risen until he touched the wounds in Jesus' hands and side.
90. The special word used to name the changing of ordinary bread and wine into the Body and Blood of Christ at the consecration at Mass.	**89.** Knowledge and customs passed on from one generation to the next.

91. vestments	**92. viaticum**
93. vice	**94. virtue**
95. vocation	**96. vow**
97. witness	**98. works of mercy**
99. worship	**100. Yahweh**

92. Holy Communion given to a person who is in danger of dying. The word means "with you on the way."

91. The special clothing worn by the priest and other ministers for liturgical celebrations.

94. A positive moral habit; a pattern of behavior that leads to goodness and holiness.

93. A negative or sinful habit; a pattern of immoral behavior.

96. A solemn promise to God or to another person, often with the community present as witness.

95. A call from God to give our lives in the service of others. God's call might be to marriage, priesthood, religious life, or a committed single life.

98. Ways that Christians are expected to serve others. The service can be "for the body" (corporal works) or "for the soul" (spiritual works).

97. One who tells what he or she has seen or heard at a certain event; one who testifies to the truth.

100. The most sacred name of God in the Hebrew scriptures. The word means "I am who am" or "the One who is."

99. Public honor shown to God in prayer and liturgy; the ceremonies, prayers, and rituals by which devotion to God is expressed.

1. adultery	2. agnostic
3. Alpha and Omega	4. atheist
5. Babel	6. canon of sacred scripture
7. chastity	8. Chi Rho
9. conversion	10. encyclical

2. A person who claims that it is not possible to know if there is a God.

1. Sexual relations between two persons, at least one of whom is married to someone else.

4. A person who believes that there is no God.

3. A title for Jesus, the beginning and end of all things. (Literally the first and last letters of the Greek alphabet.)

6. The list of books the Church has declared to be the inspired word of God.

5. The Old Testament city where the people tried to outwit God by building a tower that would reach to the heavens.

8. A symbol which is used to stand for Jesus Christ. It is made from the Greek letters X and P.

7. The virtue that directs us to use God's gift of sexuality properly. It calls all people to be pure according to their state in life.

10. A formal letter written by the pope to the entire Church.

9. A change of heart; a word that means "to turn around." It refers to turning toward God and away from sin and evil.

11. euthanasia	12. excommunication
13. exorcism	14. fidelity
15. fornication	16. fortitude
17. general intercessions	18. heresy
19. Herodians	20. Hinduism

12. A severe penalty for certain sins, which cuts a person off from being a member of the Church and prohibits them from receiving the sacraments (except for reconciliation).

11. The grave sin of actively causing the death of someone who is terminally ill, disabled, or elderly.

14. Faithfulness to one's duties, responsibilities, or religious values.

13. A special prayer in which the priest, in the name of Jesus, asks that an evil spirit leave a person.

16. A virtue which helps us to do good and to overcome obstacles to doing what is right and good.

15. Sexual intercourse between an unmarried man and an unmarried woman.

18. A false teaching; the denial of Church doctrine.

17. The prayers which people offer at Mass for their needs and the needs of others. They are also called the Prayers of the Faithful.

20. The major religion of India; it is characterized by the belief in reincarnation and a supreme being with many forms and natures.

19. Members of the ruling family of Palestine during Jesus' life.

21. holocaust	**22. ichthys**
23. idolatry	**24. incense**
25. indulgence	**26. infallibility**
27. infidelity	**28. inspiration**
29. Job	**30. justice**

22. A symbol that looks like a fish, used as a secret code by the early Christians. (The Greek word for fish is an acronym for "Jesus Christ, Son ⋈◯ of God, Savior.") ⋈◯

21. The killing of thousands of Jews by the Nazis during World War II; in the Bible it is the name for a sacrificial offering that is consumed by flames.

24. A mixture of perfumes and spices which gives off sweet-smelling smoke. It is used to remind us that our prayers rise to God as smoke rises to the sky.

23. Honoring a creature in place of God.

26. The special help the Holy Spirit provides to protect the Church from error in matters of faith and morals.

25. A share in the saving merits of Christ which removes all or part of the punishment due to us because of our sins.

28. The guidance of the Holy Spirit that helped the biblical authors to write what God wanted them to, and that now helps us to understand what is written in the Bible.

27. Being unfaithful to someone or something, especially one's marriage partner.

30. A moral virtue that gives us the strength to respect the rights of others and enables us to give God and others their due.

29. An Old Testament character who is a model of patient suffering. Though all his possessions were taken away, his children died, and he suffered from terrible illness, he never cursed God.

31. Lectionary	32. Logos
33. magisterium	34. Magnificat
35. martyr	36. meditation
37. Mohammed	38. mystagogia
39. mystery	40. Mystical Body of Christ

32. Greek for "word." It is one of the names given to the Second Person of the Trinity, who is called the Word of God.

31. The book of scripture readings used at Mass. The readings are organized into a three-year repeating cycle.

34. The name we give to Mary's great prayer of praise to God after she was told she would be the mother of Jesus.

33. The responsibility of the pope, together with the bishops, to teach the Church the true meaning of what God has revealed.

36. A kind of silent prayer in which we use scripture and our imagination to help us listen to God and respond with love.

35. A person who dies for his or her faith; the word means "witness."

38. A time after baptism when newly initiated Catholic adults come to understand more about their faith.

37. The founder of the Islamic religion.

40. An image used to describe the Church as the community of those who are united with Christ and with one another like the parts of one body.

39. A truth of our faith that we cannot fully understand but that we believe anyway because God has revealed it to us.

41. natural law	42. oil of catechumens
43. oil of the sick	44. Paraclete
45. Paschal Mystery	46. patriarch
47. pharaoh	48. Pharisees
49. Protestant Reformation	50. proverbs

42. A blessed oil used by the Church in the celebration of the sacrament of baptism.

41. A core of universally binding moral precepts that can be known by human reason without any special revelation from God.

44. One of the names given to the Holy Spirit in scriptures. It means that the Spirit has been sent to be our helper and guide.

43. A blessed oil used by the Church in the celebration of the sacrament of the anointing of the sick.

46. A title used for the founding fathers of the Hebrew people; also a title used today in the Eastern Catholic churches for a bishop responsible for a large diocese.

45. The life, death, and resurrection of Jesus; the name we give to God's plan of salvation.

48. Deeply devout Jewish people who centered their everyday lives on following the laws of God to the most minute detail.

47. The title used for the rulers of ancient Egypt.

50. Short sayings that describe truths learned from experience; an Old Testament book full of such sayings.

49. The split in Christianity that began in the sixteenth century in Europe.

51. providence	**52. prudence**
53. psalm	**54. purgatory**
55. RCIA	**56. religious liberty**
57. revelation	**58. Roman Empire**
59. Ruah	**60. rubrics**

52. The moral virtue that strengthens us to know what is good and to choose it; right reason in action.

51. God's continuing care for and guidance of the whole world and each individual.

54. A word that means "purified"; the process by which a person who has died and is not yet ready for heaven grows in the love for God.

53. One of 150 sacred songs found in the Old Testament.

56. The basic human right to worship God freely according to one's own conscience.

55. Rite of Christian Initiation of Adults. It is the process used to prepare adults to become full members of the Catholic Church.

58. Territory under the political control of Rome at the time the scriptures were written.

57. The process by which God chooses to make himself known to human beings through creation, the scriptures, and the teachings of the Church.

60. The directions that guide a Christian ritual; they are often written in red type in the ritual books.

59. A Hebrew word that means spirit, wind, and breath; it is used as a name for the Holy Spirit, the Third Person of the Trinity.

61. Sadducees	62. salvation history
63. Sanhedrin	64. schism
65. scribes	66. Seder
67. self-denial	68. St. Augustine
69. St. Bernadette	70. St. Dominic

62. The story of God's loving actions on behalf of humans, beginning with creation and lasting until the end of time.

61. A priestly sect of Judaism in Jesus' time that only accepted the written Mosaic law.

64. A division between two groups of believers.

63. The Jewish high court during the time of Jesus.

66. The special meal with which Jewish people celebrate the feast of Passover. The foods eaten symbolize their passage from slavery to freedom.

65. Jewish leaders who studied the law of God and commented on the scriptures to help others understand them.

68. One of the Church's great theologians; a Church doctor; the son of St. Monica.

67. A willingness to sacrifice one's own wants, desires, or interests for a greater good.

70. The founder of the "order of preachers"; the person who taught the Church to pray the rosary.

69. A peasant girl who received visions of the Virgin Mary at Lourdes, France.

71. St. Ignatius of Loyola	**72. St. Thérèse of Lisieux**
73. St. Thomas More	**74. St. Valentine**
75. stewardship	**76. synod**
77. synoptic gospels	**78. temperance**
79. Torah	**80. Zealots**

72. A young Carmelite sister who taught the "little way" to holiness—doing everyday things with great love for God.

71. A former Spanish soldier who founded the Jesuit order.

74. The legendary patron of lovers.

73. The English chancellor who was martyred because he refused to sign an oath to King Henry VIII.

76. A gathering of bishops meeting to advise the pope on important Church matters.

75. The responsibility of caring for someone else's property.

78. The moral virtue that helps us exercise self-control in our desires.

77. The gospels of Matthew, Mark, and Luke, which are very similar because they were derived from the same source.

80. A Jewish group that acted with force to overthrow the Romans.

79. The Jewish law, based on the first five books of the Hebrew Scriptures.

1. Recite the Sign of the Cross.

2. Recite the first half of the Hail Mary.

3. Recite the second half of the Hail Mary.

4. Recite the first half of the Our Father.

5. Recite the second half of the Our Father.

6. Name the four gospels.

7. Name the five authors of the New Testament epistles.

8. Name the seven sacraments.

9. Name the four marks of the Church.

10. Name the three theological virtues.

2. Hail Mary, full of grace, the Lord is with you. Blessed are you among women, and blessed is the fruit of your womb, Jesus.

1. In the name of the Father, and of the Son, and of the Holy Spirit. Amen.

4. Our Father, who art in heaven, hallowed be thy name. Thy kingdom come, thy will be done, on earth as it is in heaven.

3. Holy Mary, Mother of God, pray for us sinners, now and at the hour of our death. Amen.

6. Matthew, Mark, Luke, and John

5. Give us this day our daily bread and forgive us our trespasses as we forgive those who trespass against us. And lead us not into temptation, but deliver us from evil. Amen.

8. baptism, confirmation, Holy Eucharist, reconciliation (penance), anointing of the sick, holy orders, matrimony

7. Paul, James, Peter, John, Jude

10. faith, hope, and charity (love)

9. one, holy, catholic, apostolic

11. Name the three languages in which the scriptures were originally written.

12. Name the seven gifts of the Holy Spirit.

13. Name six of the twelve fruits of the Holy Spirit.

14. Name the four cardinal (moral) virtues.

15. Name the twelve apostles.

16. Name the three traditional vows taken by religious men and women.

17. Name the four major prophets of the Old Testament.

18. Name the seven capital sins.

19. Name the first five books of the Old Testament (Torah or Pentateuch).

20. Name five of the individuals or groups to whom the epistles were written.

12. wisdom, understanding, knowledge, right judgment, courage, reverence, wonder and awe in God's presence	11. Hebrew, Greek, Aramaic
14. prudence, justice, fortitude, temperance	13. love, kindness, joy, peace, patience, generosity, faithfulness, gentleness, self-control, goodness, long-suffering, chastity
16. poverty, chastity, obedience	15. Simon Peter and Andrew, James and John, Philip and Bartholomew, Thomas and Matthew, James and Thaddeus (or Jude), Simon and Judas (see Matthew 10)
18. pride, greed, lust, anger, gluttony, envy, sloth	17. Isaiah, Jeremiah, Ezekiel, Daniel
20. Romans, Corinthians, Galatians, Ephesians, Philippians, Colossians, Thessalonians, Timothy, Titus, Philemon, Hebrews	19. Genesis, Exodus, Leviticus, Numbers, Deuteronomy

ADAM	ABRAHAM
ANDREW	AMOS
ANOINTING OF THE SICK	ANNA
BARABBAS	BAPTISM

BARTHOLOMEW	BETHANY	BREAD OF LIFE	CONFIRMATION
BATHSHEBA	BETHLEHEM	CANA	COURAGE

DEBORAH

ELIZABETH

EMMAUS

EVE

DAVID

ELISHA

EMMANUEL

ESTHER

GABRIEL	GOLIATH	GOOD SHEPHERD	HERODIAS
GALILEE	GOOD SAMARITAN	HEROD	HOLY EUCHARIST

ISAAC

JACOB

JAMES (THE LESSER)

JERICHO

HOLY ORDERS

ISAIAH

JAMES (THE GREATER)

JEREMIAH

JONATHON

JOHN
THE BAPTIST

JOANNA

JERUSALEM

JOSEPH OF
ARIMATHEA

JONAH

JOHN

JOACHIM

Flash Cards

JOSHUA	JUDITH	LAMB OF GOD	LEAH
JOSEPH OF NAZARETH	JUDAS ISCARIOT	KNOWLEDGE	LAZARUS

LIGHT OF THE
WORLD

LUKE

MARY AND
MARTHA

MARY, MOTHER
OF JAMES

LOST SHEEP

MARK

MARY
MAGDALENE

MARY, MOTHER
OF JESUS

MESSIAH	MATRIMONY
MIRIAM	MICHAEL
NATHAN	MUSTARD SEED
NICODEMUS	NAZARETH

NOAH	PHILIP	PRODIGAL SON	RAPHAEL
PEARL OF GREAT PRICE	PILATE	RACHEL	REBECCA

REVERENCE

RUTH

SAMUEL

SAUL

RECONCILIATION

RIGHT JUDGMENT

SAMARIA

SARAH

THADDAEUS (JUDE)	SOWER AND SEED	SOLOMON	SIMON PETER
THE CHRIST	TEN VIRGINS	SON OF GOD	SIMON THE ZEALOT

UNDERSTANDING

WISDOM

ZACCHAEUS

THOMAS

WEDDING FEAST

WONDER AND AWE
IN GOD'S PRESENCE

ZACHARY

We believe in God, the Father almighty,	**creator of heaven and earth.**
We believe in Jesus Christ,	**his only Son, our Lord.**
He was conceived by the power of the Holy Spirit	**and born of the Virgin Mary.**
He suffered under Pontius Pilate,	**was crucified, died, and was buried.**
He descended to the dead.	**On the third day, he rose again.**

2 We believe that the whole world was made by God as a gift to be appreciated and cared for by God's children.	**1** We believe that God the Father is all powerful and that he cares for us like a loving parent.
4 We believe that Jesus is truly the Son of God, and that he is our Master and Savior.	**3** We believe that Jesus lived on earth and taught us how to know and love the Father.
6 We believe that God chose Mary to be the Mother of his Son and that she remained a virgin before and after Jesus was born.	**5** We believe that the Holy Spirit, not a human man, caused Jesus to begin to grow in Mary's womb.
8 We believe that Jesus was nailed to a cross, died a painful death, and was buried in a new tomb by his friends.	**7** We believe that the civil leaders in Jerusalem made the decision to have Jesus punished and killed.
10 We believe that Jesus rose from the dead on Easter Sunday morning.	**9** We believe that after Jesus died he went down to the realm of the dead and opened the gates of heaven for those who had died before him.

He ascended into heaven,	and is seated at the right hand of the Father.
He will come again to judge the living and the dead.	We believe in the Holy Spirit,
the holy catholic Church,	the communion of saints,
the forgiveness of sins,	the resurrection of the body,
and life everlasting.	Amen.

12
We believe that Jesus is now in heaven where he shares power and glory with the Father and the Holy Spirit.

11
We believe that the glorified body of Jesus was taken into heaven.

14
We believe that the Spirit of God is poured into our hearts by Jesus.

13
We believe that Jesus will come at the end of time to reward those who love him and to punish those who have rejected his love.

16
We believe in the unity of all people who love Jesus: those still living on earth, those suffering in purgatory, and those already in heaven.

15
We believe that Jesus established his Church to lead all people to God.

18
We believe that our bodies will return to life and be reunited with our souls at the end of time.

17
We believe that Jesus gave his Church the power to forgive sins, and that he asks us to forgive one another.

20
We accept God's word, God's promises, God's commandments, and we entrust our lives completely to God.

19
We believe that those who died in God's grace and friendship will live with God in heaven for ever.

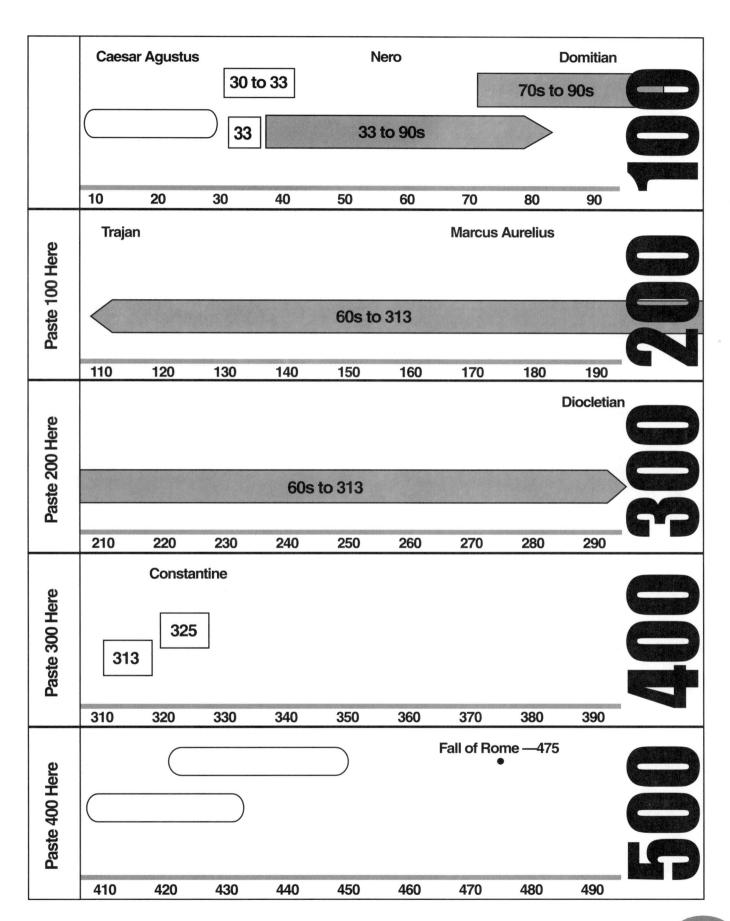

Caesar Agustus **Nero** **Domitian**

30 to 33

70s to 90s

33   33 to 90s

10 20 30 40 50 60 70 80 90 **100**

Trajan **Marcus Aurelius**

60s to 313

110 120 130 140 150 160 170 180 190 **200**

Diocletian

60s to 313

210 220 230 240 250 260 270 280 290 **300**

Constantine

325

313

310 320 330 340 350 360 370 380 390 **400**

Fall of Rome —475
●

410 420 430 440 450 460 470 480 490 **500**

Paste 100 Here
Paste 200 Here
Paste 300 Here
Paste 400 Here

Paste 500 Here

600

| 510 | 520 | 530 | 540 | 550 | 560 | 570 | 580 | 590 |

Paste 600 Here

Mohammed and the Spread of Islam →

700

| 610 | 620 | 630 | 640 | 650 | 660 | 670 | 680 | 690 |

Paste 700 Here

Battle of Tours - 732
●

800

| 710 | 720 | 730 | 740 | 750 | 760 | 770 | 780 | 790 |

Paste 800 Here

800

900

| 810 | 820 | 830 | 840 | 850 | 860 | 870 | 880 | 890 |

Paste 900 Here

Leif Ericson - 1000 ●

1000

| 910 | 920 | 930 | 940 | 950 | 960 | 970 | 980 | 990 |

Who, What, When Time Line

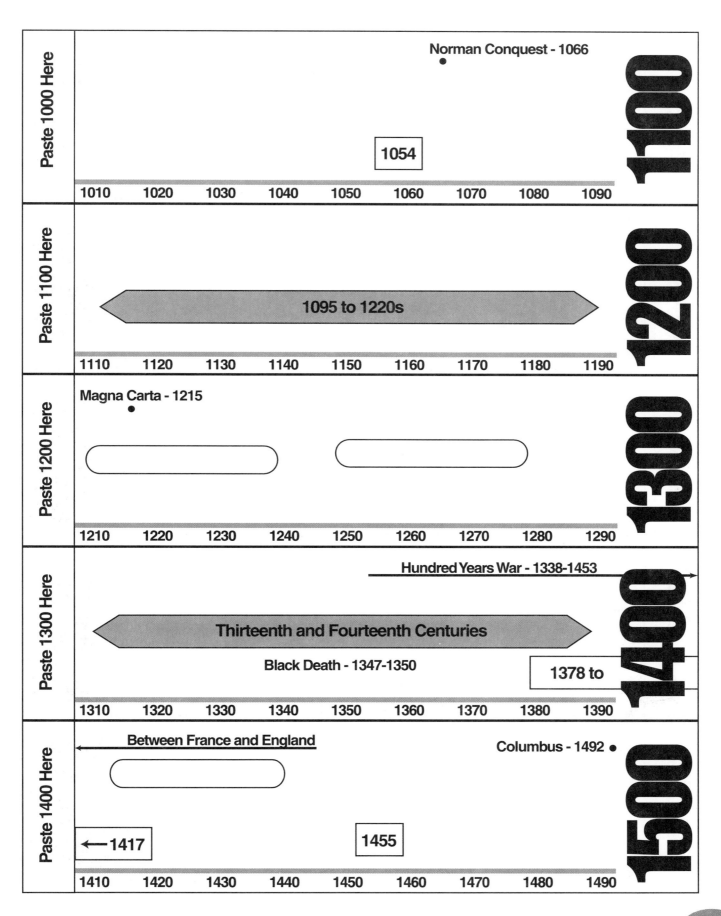

Paste 1000 Here

Norman Conquest - 1066 •

1054

1010 1020 1030 1040 1050 1060 1070 1080 1090

1100

Paste 1100 Here

1095 to 1220s

1110 1120 1130 1140 1150 1160 1170 1180 1190

1200

Paste 1200 Here

Magna Carta - 1215 •

1210 1220 1230 1240 1250 1260 1270 1280 1290

1300

Paste 1300 Here

Hundred Years War - 1338-1453

Thirteenth and Fourteenth Centuries

Black Death - 1347-1350

1378 to

1310 1320 1330 1340 1350 1360 1370 1380 1390

1400

Paste 1400 Here

← Between France and England

Columbus - 1492 •

← 1417

1455

1410 1420 1430 1440 1450 1460 1470 1480 1490

1500

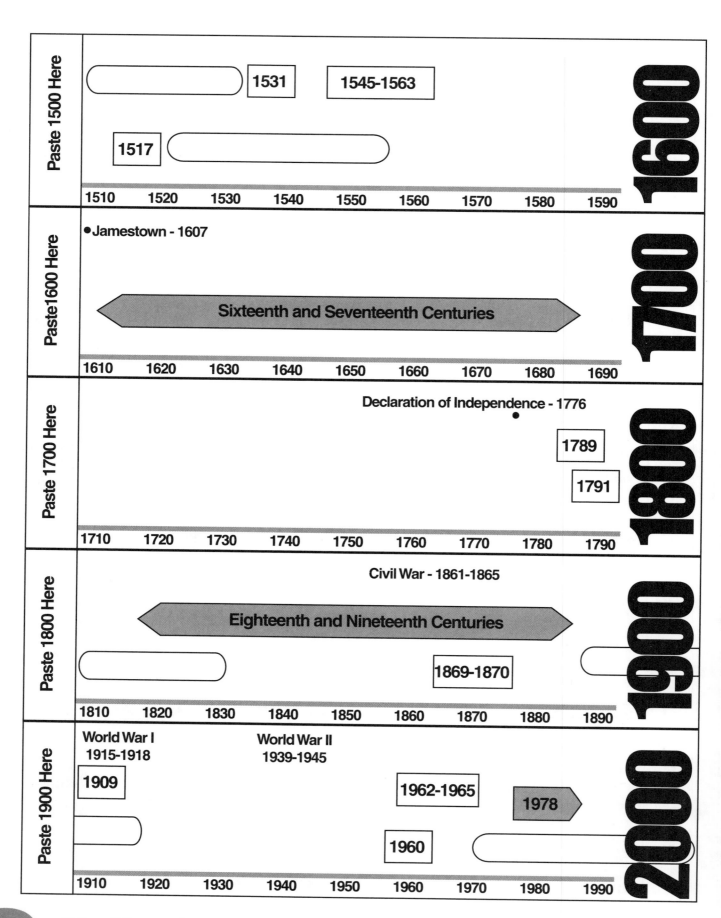

Paste 1500 Here

1531

1545-1563

1517

1510 1520 1530 1540 1550 1560 1570 1580 1590

1600

Paste 1600 Here

• Jamestown - 1607

Sixteenth and Seventeenth Centuries

1610 1620 1630 1640 1650 1660 1670 1680 1690

1700

Paste 1700 Here

Declaration of Independence - 1776

1789

1791

1710 1720 1730 1740 1750 1760 1770 1780 1790

1800

Paste 1800 Here

Civil War - 1861-1865

Eighteenth and Nineteenth Centuries

1869-1870

1810 1820 1830 1840 1850 1860 1870 1880 1890

1900

Paste 1900 Here

World War I
1915-1918

World War II
1939-1945

1909

1962-1965

1978

1960

1910 1920 1930 1940 1950 1960 1970 1980 1990

2000

Who, What, When Time Line

Jesus of Nazareth

Jesus is born in Bethlehem and grows up in Nazareth in the home of Mary and the carpenter Joseph.

Public Life of Jesus

Jesus heals the sick, gives sight to the blind, and preaches a message of love and forgiveness. He calls twelve men, called apostles, to be his special followers.

Death and Resurrection of Jesus

Jesus is condemned as a criminal and crucified. Three days later he rises from the dead.

Early Church Beginnings

The apostles carry the message of Jesus throughout the Mediterranean world, establishing churches in places like Rome, Corinth, Ephesus, Philippi, and Galatia.

Gospels Written

The early Christian communities preserve the memories and teachings of Jesus in the four gospel accounts: Matthew, Mark, Luke, and John.

Persecutions

The Roman Emperors proclaim Christianity to be illegal. Christians who refuse to worship the pagan gods are tortured, exiled, imprisoned, burned, or thrown to the lions.

Edict of Milan

Emperor Constantine proclaims religious freedom for all, making the Christian religion legal. Christians come up from the catacombs and begin to build churches where they can worship openly.

Council of Nicea

The first ecumenical council is held. All the bishops of the Church come together to write a statement of Christian belief called the Nicene Creed. This creed is still recited at Mass each Sunday.

St. Augustine

After living a wild life, Augustine converts to Christianity. He becomes the Bishop of Hippo in Northern Africa and one of the greatest leaders and scholars of the Church.

St. Patrick

Patrick brings Christianity to Ireland. In the years to come, Ireland will become a major center of Christian learning and faith.

30 to 33	**First Century**
33 to 90s	**33**
60s to 313	**70s to 90s**
325	**313**
Early Fifth Century	**Early Fifth Century**

Who, What, When Study Cards

St. Benedict

Benedict draws up a rule of life for monks which is still followed today. Men and women who live by this rule are called Benedictines.

St. Boniface

Boniface, a missionary from England, brings Christianity to Germany.

Charlemagne Crowned Emperor

Charlemagne is crowned the first emperor of the Holy Roman Empire. He promotes good laws and education throughout the empire.

Sts. Cyril and Methodius

Cyril and Methodius bring Christianity to central Europe. They are known as the "Apostles of the Slavs" and later as the patron saints of all Europe.

The East-West Schism

A split occurs between the Eastern Church (based in Constantinople) and the Western Church (based in Rome). The schism has never been completely healed.

Crusades

A series of "holy wars" are fought in an effort to win back the Holy Land from the control of Moslems.

Sts. Francis and Clare

Francis founds an order of brothers in Assisi, Italy, dedicated to living lives of simplicity and poverty like Jesus; he is soon followed by Clare, who founds an order of sisters.

St. Thomas Aquinas

Thomas Aquinas, a Dominican friar, writes his great work, *The Summa Theologica*, a summary of all theological teaching.

Gothic Cathedrals

Great gothic cathedrals are built to praise God, featuring huge spires and glorious stained glass windows. Many of these cathedrals still stand in Europe in places like Chartres, France, and Cologne, Germany.

Rival Popes

A period of crisis arises in which two (and later three) rivals claim to be pope. St. Catherine of Siena helps to restore unity.

Eighth Century	Sixth Century
Ninth Century	800
1095 to 1200's	1054
Late Thirteenth Century	Early Thirteenth Century
1378 to 1417	Thirteenth and Fourteenth Centuries

Who, What, When, Study Cards

St. Joan of Arc

A peasant girl named Joan hears a call from God to lead the French army against the English. She is taken prisoner by the English, accused of being a witch, and burned at the stake.

Gutenberg Bible

The Bible is printed for the first time on a movable printing press, making it more available to the common people.

Michelangelo

The great artist and sculptor Michelangelo is commissioned by the pope to paint the ceiling of the Sistine Chapel in Rome.

St. Ignatius of Loyola

Ignatius, a former soldier, founds a community of men to serve the Church. They are called the Society of Jesus, or Jesuits.

Protestant Reformation

A German monk, Martin Luther, begins the Protestant Reformation by nailing a letter of protest against the Church to a cathedral door. Other reformers follow.

Our Lady of Guadalupe

Mary appears to Juan Diego, a simple peasant, in Mexico. She leaves her image imprinted on his cloak. Our Lady of Guadalupe comes to be called the Patroness of the Americas.

Council of Trent

An ecumenical council is called in response to the Protestant Reformation. It clarifies the difference between Catholic doctrine and the teachings of the reform churches.

Missionaries to the Americas

Christian missionaries from Europe come to America to preach to the native tribes. Some of the natives are converted, others attack and kill the missionaries. One of the converts, Kateri Tekakwitha, will be declared blessed and considered for sainthood.

Immigration to America

Large groups of Catholics immigrate to the New World, bringing with them priests and religious who start parishes, schools, and hospitals throughout America.

First American Bishop

John Carroll is named the first American bishop. His diocese, with headquarters in Baltimore, includes the whole United States.

1455	**Fifteenth Century**
Early Sixteenth Century	**Early Sixteenth Century**
1531	**1517**
Sixteenth and Seventeenth Centuries	**1545 to 1563**
1789	**Eighteenth and Nineteenth Centuries**

Who, What, When Study Cards

Religious Freedom

The First Amendment of the U.S. Constitution is written, guaranteeing religious freedom for all Americans.

St. Elizabeth Ann Seton

Elizabeth Ann Seton founds the first American order of sisters, the Sisters of Charity, devoted to educating poor children. She will become the first American-born saint.

First Vatican Council

The bishops of the world declare that the pope is infallible when teaching matters of faith and morals.

Rerum Novarum

Pope Leo XII issues an encyclical letter in support of the rights of workers to a just wage and healthy working conditions. It is the first of several social encyclicals to be written by the popes.

St. Frances Cabrini

Mother Cabrini establishes hospitals, schools, and orphanages for poor immigrants throughout the United States and in Central and South Americas.

Children's Communion

Pope Pius X changes the age for First Eucharist, allowing children as young as seven to receive communion.

Catholic President

John F. Kennedy is elected president of the United States, the first time a Catholic has been chosen for this high office.

Second Vatican Council

Pope John XXIII calls an ecumenical council which makes major changes in the Church, especially in the celebration of Eucharist and the other sacraments.

Mother Teresa of Calcutta

Mother Teresa founds the Missionaries of Charity to care for the dying poor in Calcutta, India. The order now has thousands of members and serves the poorest of the poor in all parts of the world.

Pope John Paul II Elected

Karol Wojtyla becomes the first Polish man to be elected pope. As pope he travels extensively, bringing a message of faith and courage, especially to young people.

Early Nineteenth Century	**1791**
1891	**1869 to 1870**
1909	**Early Twentieth Century**
1962 to 1965	**1960**
1978	**Late Twentieth Century**

Who, What, When Study Cards

Seq	Date	Word	Definition
1	First Century	Jesus of Nazareth	Jesus is born in Bethlehem and grows up in Nazareth in the home of Mary and the carpenter Joseph.
2	30 to 33	Public Life of Jesus	Jesus heals the sick, gives sight to the blind, and preaches a message of love and forgiveness. He calls twelve men, called apostles, to be his special followers.
3	33	Death and Resurrection of Jesus	Jesus is condemned as a criminal and crucified. Three days later he rises from the dead.
4	33 to 90s	Early Church beginnings	The apostles carry the message of Jesus throughout the Mediterranean world, establishing churches in places like Rome, Corinth, Ephesus, Philippi, and Galatia.
5	70s to 90s	Gospels Written	The early Christian communities preserve the memories and teachings of Jesus in the four gospel accounts: Matthew, Mark, Luke, and John.
6	60s to 313	Persecutions	The Roman Emperors proclaim Christianity to be illegal. Christians who refuse to worship the pagan gods are tortured, exiled, imprisoned, burned, or thrown to the lions.
7	313	Edict of Milan	Emperor Constantine proclaims religious freedom for all, making the Christian religion legal. Christians come up from the catacombs and begin to build churches where they can worship openly.
8	325	Council of Nicea	The first ecumenical council is held. All the bishops of the Church come together to write a statement of Christian belief called the Nicene Creed. This creed is still recited at Mass each Sunday.
9	Early Fifth Century	St. Augustine	After living a wild life, Augustine converts to Christianity. He becomes the Bishop of Hippo in Northern Africa and one of the greatest leaders and scholars of the Church.
10	Early Fifth Century	St. Patrick	Patrick brings Christianity to Ireland. In the years to come, Ireland will become a major center of Christian learning and faith.

Seq	Date	Word	Definition
11	Sixth Century	St. Benedict	Benedict draws up a rule of life for monks which is still followed today. Men and women who live by this rule are called Benedictines.
12	Eighth Century	St. Boniface	Boniface, a missionary from England, brings Christianity to Germany.
13	800	Charlemagne Crowned Emperor	Charlemagne is crowned the first emperor of the Holy Roman Empire. He promotes good laws and education throughout the empire.
14	Ninth Century	Sts. Cyril and Methodius	Cyril and Methodius bring Christianity to central Europe. They are known as the "Apostles of the Slavs" and later as the patron saints of all Europe.
15	1054	The East-West Schism	A split occurs between the Eastern Church (based in Constantinople) and the Western Church (based in Rome). The schism has never been completely healed.
16	1095 to 1200s	Crusades	A series of "holy wars" are fought in an effort to win back the Holy Land from the control of Moslems.
17	Early Thirteenth Century	Sts. Francis and Clare	Francis founds an order of brothers in Assisi, Italy, dedicated to living lives of simplicity and poverty like Jesus; he is soon followed by Clare, who founds an order of sisters.
18	Late Thirteenth Century	St. Thomas Aquinas	Thomas Aquinas, a Dominican friar, writes his great work, *The Summa Theologica*, a summary of all theological teaching.
19	Thirteenth and Fourteenth Centuries	Gothic Cathedrals	Great gothic cathedrals are built to praise God, featuring huge spires and glorious stained glass windows. Many of these cathedrals still stand in Europe in places like Chartres, Frane, and Cologne, Germany.
20	1378 to 1417	Rival Popes	A period of crisis arises in which two (and later three) rivals claim to be pope. St. Catherine of Siena helps to restore unity.

Seq	Date	Word	Definition
21	Fifteenth Century	St. Joan of Arc	A peasant girl named Joan hears a call from God to lead the French army against the English. She is taken prisoner, accused of being a witch, and burned at the stake.
22	1455	Gutenberg Bible	The Bible is printed for the first time on a movable printing press, making it more available to the common people.
23	Early Sixteenth Century	Michelangelo	The great artist and sculptor Michelangelo is commissioned by the pope to paint the ceiling of the Sistine Chapel in Rome.
24	Early Sixteenth Century	St. Ignatius of Loyola	Ignatius, a former soldier, founds a community of men to serve the Church. They are called the Society of Jesus, or Jesuits.
25	1517	Protestant Reformation	A German monk, Martin Luther, begins the Protestant Reformation by nailing a letter of protest against the Church to a cathedral door. Other reformers follow.
26	1531	Our Lady of Guadalupe	Mary appears to Juan Diego, a simple peasant, in Mexico. She leaves her image imprinted on his cloak. Our Lady of Guadalupe comes to be called the Patroness of the Americas.
27	1545 to 1563	Council of Trent	An ecumenical council is called in response to the Protestant Reformation. It clarifies the difference between Catholic doctrine and the teachings of the reform churches.
28	Sixteenth and Seventeenth Centuries	Missionaries to the Americas	Christian missionaries from Europe come to America to preach to the native tribes. Some of the natives are converted, others attack and kill the missionaries. One of the converts, Kateri Tekakwitha, will be declared blessed and considered for sainthood.
29	Eighteenth and Nineteenth Centuries	Immigration to America	Large groups of Catholics immigrate to the New World, bringing with them priests and religious who start parishes, schools, and hospitals throughout America.
30	1789	First American Bishop	John Carroll is named the first American bishop. His diocese, with headquarters in Baltimore, includes the whole United States.

Seq	Date	Word	Definition
31	1791	**Religious Freedom**	The First Amendment of the U.S. Constitution is written, guaranteeing religious freedom for all Americans.
32	Early Nineteenth Century	**St. Elizabeth Ann Seton**	Elizabeth Ann Seton founds the first American order of sisters, the Sisters of Charity, devoted to educating poor children. She will become the first American-born saint.
33	1869 to 1870	**First Vatican Council**	The bishops of the world declare that the pope is infallible when teaching matters of faith and morals.
34	1891	*Rerum Novarum*	Pope Leo XII issues an encyclical letter in support of the rights of workers to a just wage and healthy working conditions. It is the first of several social encyclicals to be written by the popes.
35	Early Twentieth Century	**St. Frances Cabrini**	Mother Cabrini establishes hospitals, schools, and orphanages for poor immigrants throughout the United States and in Central and South Americas.
36	1909	**Children's Communion**	Pope Pius X changes the age for First Eucharist, allowing children as young as seven to receive communion.
37	1960	**Catholic President**	John F. Kennedy is elected president of the United States, the first time a Catholic has been chosen for this high office.
38	1962 to 1965	**Second Vatican Council**	Pope John XXIII calls an ecumenical council which makes major changes in the Church, especially in the celebration of Eucharist and the other sacraments.
39	Late Twentieth Century	**Mother Teresa of Calcutta**	Mother Teresa founds the Missionaries of Charity to care for the dying poor in Calcutta, India. The order now has thousands of members and serves the poorest of the poor in all parts of the world.
40	1978	**Pope John Paul II Elected**	Karol Wojtyla becomes the first Polish man to be elected pope. As pope he travels extensively, bringing a message of faith and courage, especially to young people.

Who, What, When Date Sheets

1. The first creation story tells us that God created man and woman to resemble someone. Who?

GENESIS 1:26-28

2. According to the first creation account, what did God do on the seventh day?

GENESIS 2:1-3

3. Eve was given her name by her husband, Adam. Adam's name means "the man." What does Eve's name mean?

GENESIS 3:20

4. The first two sons of Adam and Eve were called Cain and Abel. What work did each do?

GENESIS 4:2

5. Who designed the ark that Noah built?

GENESIS 6:11-16

6. According to the story of the great flood, how many human beings were on the ark?

GENESIS 8:13

7. Abraham had two sons, the first born to his wife's maid Hagar, the second to his wife Sarah. Name the two boys.

GENESIS 16:15; 21:3

8. When God threatened to destroy the city of Sodom, Abraham tried to bargain with him to spare the city. What deal did he offer God?

GENESIS 18:22-32

9. God tested Abraham's faith by asking him to sacrifice his son Issac. What was Abraham's reward for being willing to do so?

GENESIS 22:15-18

10. Abraham sent his servants back to his own homeland to find a wife for his son Issac. Who did they bring back for him?

GENESIS 24:1-66

11. Jacob and Esau were the twin sons of Rebecca. Who was their father?

GENESIS 25:24-26

12. When Jacob's son Joseph was a teenager he was sold into slavery by his older brothers. Why did they do this to him?

GENESIS 37:1-28

13. When a great famine came over the land of Israel, Jacob sent his older sons to Egypt to buy grain. Who was in charge of the grain supply there?

GENESIS 42:6

14. When Moses was a tiny baby, his mother placed him in a basket which she hid in the reeds beside the river. Who found him there?

EXODUS 2:1-10

15. God spoke to Moses and told him to lead God's people out of Egypt. Moses then asked God to tell him his name. What was God's answer?

EXODUS 3:11-14

16. Every year Jewish people everywhere celebrate the feast of Passover. What event in their history does this feast commemorate?

EXODUS 12:24-27

17. What important message did God reveal to Moses on Mount Sinai?

EXODUS 19—29

18. When Moses came down from the mountain carrying the stone tablets, he found the people worshiping a golden calf. What did he do then?

EXODUS 32:15-20

19. As the Israelites traveled through the desert on their way to the Promised Land, what was their sign that God was always with them?

EXODUS 40:38

20. The greatest of the commandments in the Old Testaments is called the "Shema." What are the words of this commandment?

EXODUS 6:4-9

21. The Ten Commandments are found in both Exodus and Deuteronomy. Exodus calls the place where they were revealed Mount Sinai. What does Deuteronomy call this place?

DEUTERONOMY 5:1-21

22. After Moses died, who did God choose to lead the Israelites into the Promised Land?

JOSHUA 1:1-6

23. When Samuel was still a boy, he heard God call him in the night. What answer did he give to God?

1 SAMUEL 3:8-10

24. When David was a young lad, he saved his people from a powerful giant. Name the giant and tell how David killed him.

1 SAMUEL 17:1-51

25. The Old Testament tells about a deep friendship between the son of King Saul and one of Saul's squires. Name the friends.

1 SAMUEL 18:1-5

26. The prophet Nathan told King David a parable about a rich man who took the only lamb of a poor man to make a meal for his guests. What did the parable mean?

2 SAMUEL 11—12

27. Solomon became the king of Israel after his father David died. What special gift did he ask for and receive from God?

1 KINGS 3:7-12

28. King Solomon used his wisdom to solve a difficult case involving two women who both claimed to be the mother of an infant. How did he resolve the case?

1 KINGS 3:16-18

29. Which king of Israel built the Temple in Jerusalem?

1 KINGS 6:1-18

30. According to the scriptures, how was the prophet Elijah taken to heaven?

2 KINGS 2:9-12

31. Naaman was an army commander who came to the prophet Elisha to be cured of leprosy. What was the cure prescribed by Elisha?

2 KINGS 5:1-14

32. The Bible tells about a great many sufferings and losses endured by the man named Job. What was Job's response to all of these trials?

JOB 2:21

33. The books of Maccabees tell of a whole family—a mother and her seven sons—who were executed by the king. What was their crime?

2 MACCABEES 7:1-3

34. What title is given to God in the famous Twenty-Third Psalm?

PSALM 23:1

35. The book of Proverbs gives a long description of the "ideal wife." Name at least five things she does well.

PROVERBS 21:10-28

36. The prophet Jeremiah received a message from God as he watched a potter working at his wheel. What was the message?

JEREMIAH 18:1-8

37. The prophet Ezekiel had a vision in which he saw a field full of bones. What happened when he prayed over the bones?

EZEKIEL 37:1-14

38. In the book of Daniel we are told about three young men who refused to worship a golden statue. What did the king do to punish them?

DANIEL 3:1-24

39. When the prophet Daniel was still a young boy, God sent him to save the beautiful Susanna from execution. Of what had she been accused?

DANIEL 13:1-42

40. The prophet Micah tells us that God asks us to do only three things. What are they?

MICAH 6:8

Old Testament Trivia Cards

1. How old was the young girl Jesus brought back to life?

MARK 5:42

2. Which apostle said he would not believe in the resurrection unless he could put his fingers in Jesus' nail prints?

JOHN 20:24-25

3. On the day of the resurrection, Jesus ate supper with his disciples in a town seven miles from Jerusalem. Name the town.

LUKE 24:13

4. On Easter morning, who was the first person to discover that the stone had been rolled away and the tomb was empty?

JOHN 20:1

5. Name both parents of John the Baptist.

LUKE 1:5-23

6. The disciples wanted to know why a man had been born blind. Was it to punish his parents, they asked. What was Jesus' answer?

JOHN 9:1-3

7. Jesus praised a poor widow for the offering she put into the collection box. How much did she give?

MARK 12:42

8. Who was the Roman emperor when Jesus was born?

LUKE 2:1

9. The gospels tell of a woman who was cured by touching the hem of Jesus' cloak. What was she cured of?

LUKE 8:43

10. After his arrest, Jesus was tried by several different authority figures. Which one of them ordered him to be whipped?

LUKE 23:13-16

11. Name the Pharisee who came secretly at night to learn from Jesus.

JOHN 3:1

12. Name the rich man who wrapped the body of Jesus in a linen sheet and placed it in his own tomb.

MATTHEW 27:57-60

13. At whose request did Jesus change the water into wine at the wedding at Cana?

JOHN 2:6-11

14. What words were nailed to the cross above Jesus' head?

MATTHEW 27:37

15. What special responsibility did Judas have in the little band of apostles?

JOHN 13:29

16. When Jesus was dying on the cross, what words did he speak to his young friend John?

JOHN 19:27

17. What job did Matthew have before he was called to follow Jesus?

MATTHEW 9:9

18. Judas returned the thirty pieces of silver he got for betraying Jesus. What did the chief priests do with the money?

MATTHEW 27:7

19. What story did Jesus tell in response to the question: "Who is my neighbor?"

LUKE 10:29-37

20. In what town did the people reject Jesus' teaching and try to throw him off the cliff?

LUKE 4:16, 29

Gospel Trivia Cards

21. Name the little tax collector who climbed a tree so he could see Jesus passing by.

LUKE 19:2-3

22. Who was the criminal who was released to the crowd by Pilate at Jesus' trial?

MATTHEW 27:16, 20

23. How many baskets of scraps did the apostles collect after they had fed the 5,000 people?

MATTHEW 14:20

24. Jesus often stayed at the home of his good friends, Mary, Martha, and Lazarus. In what town did they live?

JOHN 11:1

25. Two of the apostles were sons of a man named Zebedee. Name the sons.

MATTHEW 10:2

26. Jesus was crucified at a place called Golgotha. What does the name Golgotha mean?

MATTHEW 27:33

27. How often does Jesus say we should forgive a person who offends us?

MATTHEW 18:22

28. On what day of the week did Jesus cure a man's paralyzed hand?

MARK 3:1-6

29. According to Matthew's gospel, what are the very last words Jesus says to his friends before he ascends into heaven?

MATTHEW 28:20

30. Jesus cures a relative of one of the apostles. Name the apostle and the relative.

MATTHEW 8:14-15

31. How did Jesus answer the Jews who asked if they ought to pay taxes to Rome?

MARK 12:13-17

36. Jesus tells a story about ten wise virgins and ten foolish virgins. In the story, what do the foolish girls run out of?

MATTHEW 25:3

32. Three of Jesus' favorite disciples were with him at his transfiguration and again during his agony in the garden. Name them.

MARK 9:2-4; 14:32-35

37. When the prodigal son returned home, his father threw a big party for him. Name three things he wore to the party.

LUKE 15:22

33. In the parable of the sower, what does the seed stand for?

LUKE 8:11-15

38. When Jesus was being arrested in the garden, one of the apostles injured the slave of the high priest. What was the injury?

LUKE 22:49

34. Once a group of men couldn't get their paralyzed friend close to Jesus because of the crowd in the house. What was their solution to the problem?

MARK 2:1-5

39. What person did Jesus cure at the request of a Roman soldier?

MATTHEW 8:6

35. Jesus tells a story about a poor beggar who lay at the gate of a rich man. In the story the beggar goes to heaven and the rich man goes to hell. Name the beggar.

LUKE 16:20

40. Who does Jesus say we should invite to our parties? The gospel names four groups. Name at least three of them.

LUKE 14:13

Beatitude List

1. **Blessed are the poor in spirit,**   **for theirs is the kingdom of heaven.**

2. **Blessed are those who mourn,**   **for they will be comforted.**

3. **Blessed are the meek,**   **for they will inherit the earth.**

4. **Blessed are those who hunger and thirst for righteousness,**   **for they will be satisfied.**

5. **Blessed are the merciful,**   **for they will be shown mercy.**

6. **Blessed are the clean of heart,**   **for they will see God.**

7. **Blessed are the peacemakers,**   **for they will be called the children of God.**

8. **Blessed are they who are persecuted for the sake of righteousness,**   **for theirs is the kingdom of heaven.**

Blessed are those
who mourn,

Blessed are those who hunger and
thirst for righteousness,

Blessed are the clean
of heart,

Blessed are they who are
persecuted for the sake of
righteousness,

Blessed are the poor in spirit,

Blessed are the meek,

Blessed are the merciful,

Blessed are
the peacemakers,

for they will be comforted.

for they will be satisfied.

for they will see God.

for theirs is the kingdom of heaven.

for theirs is the kingdom of heaven.

for they will inherit the earth.

for they will be shown mercy.

for they will be called the children of God.

Beatitude Study Cards

1 and 2 Maccabees	1 and 2 Samuel	Genesis
Job	1 and 2 Kings	Exodus
Psalms	1 and 2 Chronicles	Leviticus
Proverbs	Ezra	Numbers
Ecclesiastes	Nehemiah	Deuteronomy
Song of Songs	Tobit	Joshua
Wisdom	Judith	Judges
Sirach	Esther	Ruth

Joel	Hosea	Daniel	Ezekiel	Baruch	Lamentations	Jeremiah	Isaiah
Haggai	Zephaniah	Habakkuk	Nahum	Micah	Jonah	Obadiah	Amos
						Malachi	Zechariah

Bible Books Key Word Cards

1 and 2 Peter	Ephesians	Matthew
1, 2, and 3 John	Philippians	Mark
Jude	Colossians	Luke
Hebrews	1 and 2 Thessalonians	John
Revelation to John	1 and 2 Timothy	Acts of the Apostles
	Titus	Romans
	Philemon	1 and 2 Corinthians
	James	Galatians

Gospels

History of Early Christian Church

Letters by Paul

Other Letters

Apocalyptic

**Pentateuch
(The Torah)**

Historical Books

Wisdom Books

Prophetic Books

C	A	T	H	G	R	A	W	C	O	M	M	U	N	I
F	I	B	O	L	I	C	H	U	R	C	H	E	C	O
A	F	M	Y	U	V	E	S	Z	E	E	D	N	T	U
B	I	S	E	U	C	H	A	R	I	S	T	T	R	X
S	H	O	P	X	R	E	C	O	N	C	I	L	I	A
O	W	C	O	N	F	I	R	M	A	T	I	O	N	T
L	I	H	B	S	Z	B	A	P	T	I	S	M	S	I
U	N	R	R	O	U	L	M	V	X	D	E	A	C	O
T	E	I	E	X	H	J	E	S	U	S	W	T	A	N
I	T	S	A	N	O	I	N	T	I	N	G	E	C	A
O	L	M	D	U	L	S	T	I	A	N	O	F	P	N
N	P	N	G	E	Y	I	S	N	E	S	K	T	H	E
R	R	I	A	F	O	R	D	E	R	S	M	A	S	S
A	Y	E	S	C	H	G	I	V	W	A	T	E	R	I
M	A	T	R	I	M	O	N	Y	C	O	N	F	K	L

Sacraments Word Search

C R E D O

		FREE		